7 DIFFERENT KINDS OF VOICES

DAVID C. HAIRABEDIAN

Copyright © 2019 David C. Hairabedian

No part of this publication may be reproduced or transmitted in any form or by any means, mechanical or electronic, including photocopying and recording, or by any information storage and retrieval system, without permission in writing from author or publisher (except by a reviewer, who may quote brief passages and/or show brief video clips in a review).

FORWARD

"There are, it may be, so many kinds of voices in the world, and none of them is without signification [significance]."
(1 Corinthians 14:10 KJV)

Each day various kinds of voices contend for our attention. Some voices have our best interest in mind, while others have another agenda. We often hear the familiar voice of friends, family, and at times, the voice of an enemy. Some voices are external, other voices are internal. From outside we hear the voices of people, music, news, politicians, marketing ads, and even voices that speak into our minds from the invisible realm; both angelic and demonic. From inside we hear the voice of our own thoughts, imaginations, fleshly desires and even the joy and pain that speaks to us from our own soul. Some voices encourage us, others discourage us. Some flatter, others accuse. Whether we realize it or not we are bombarded by different kinds of voices all day, every day; each voice vies for our attention. How do we distinguish which voice to listen to? History records many wars have been won or lost based solely on the voice of an advisor or friend. Business deals, career choices, relationships, health decisions, marriage and divorce, and much more are affected by the voices we give attention to. Question? Which voice influences or advises you?

Do you want to learn how to distinguish the right voice from the wrong? This book will instruct how to recognize the proper voice and ignore and discard the others. Welcome to **Seven Different Kinds of Voices.** This begins your journey of how to accurately hear the voice of God, the One Voice Who truly wants the best for you. Hearing His voice brings freedom. Let's get started!

The Bible reveals seven primary kinds of voices. These are:

1. **Voice of God** (The Father, Son and Holy Spirit)
2. **Voice of Satan** (Satan, Devils and False Prophets)
3. **Voice of World** (Wordly Wisdom, Worldly Ways and Worldly Counsel)
4. **Voice of Flesh** (The Lust of the Flesh, Lust of the Eyes and Pride of Life)
5. **Voice of Soul** (Mind, Will and Emotions)
6. **Voice of the Dead** (Necromancy and listening to our Old Nature)
7. **Voice of Religion** (Pharisee and Sadducee voices that oppose Christ)

The most important voice of these seven is the **Voice of God.** "There are, it may be, so many kinds of voices in the world, and none of them *is* without signification [significance]." **(1 Corinthians 14:10 KJV).** Once you learn to recognize and obey God's voice, all the other voices become secondary echoes in the game of life. By hearing and following God's voice you will begin to experience victory in all that you put your hand to do. God will walk with you, direct your paths, and make your way fruitful and prosperous. In addition, His peace will fill and flood your soul. He will reveal heaven's strategies and expose the snares and trip wires of hell. As you walk with Him, He will make your way straight and your enemies will part like the red sea as you walk though in victory. You will grow in your faith and walk stronger and stronger. You will increase in authority. Your words will become His Words (1Peter 4:11). He is a supernatural God, and when you walk together, you partner with Heaven, and your life will be endued with supernatural results. You will reveal Jesus; you'll become his representative in the earth. "Christ in you, the hope of glory" (Colossians 1:27 NKJV). Jesus with skin on. This is His goal for you. You will become a conduit to release His goodness, wisdom, power, provision, love, hope, healing and miracles, to others (Mark 16:17-18). You will never be the same! If this is something you want for your life, read on.

Jesus said, **"My sheep hear my voice, and I know them, and they follow me"** (John 10:27). God's desire is that you personally hear His Voice. Hearing God's voice becomes easier over time and with practice. The good news is God designed you with the ability to hear Him. Moreover, He desires you hear Him. "My sheep hear my voice." This is His promise for all His sheep. He is your Shepherd. And He has time for each one of His children, one-on-one. He enjoys spending time with you. He is a personal God. Fellowship with Him involves two-way communication; at times it is like a dialogue between friends. At other times it is instruction from a Teacher. Other times you'll receive a prophetic word, or a revelation while spending time in His presence. At other times it's an imperative from a Commander. You will learn to hear His voice in several ways. You will sometimes even learn from Him when He remains silent.

God wants you to be His friend, and He wants to be your friend. Friendship with God is cultivated and developed over time; time with Him in prayer, quiet time listening for His voice, time spent reading His Word with revelation from the Holy Spirit, and time in worship at His feet. This book will provide you with several keys to develop a personal relationship with the Holy Spirit, where "deep calls unto deep" (Psalms 42:7). You will discover how to recognize God's voice above all the other voices of the world, and as you journey you will be transformed more and more into the image and likeness of Jesus as the Bible promises. "But we all, with open face beholding as in a glass the glory of the Lord, are changed into the same image from glory to glory, even as by the Spirit of the Lord." (2Corinthians 3:18 KJV).

The Old Testament prophet Amos declared, 'Can two walk together unless they be agreed?' (Amos 3:3 KJV). When we walk with God, we begin to agree with Him. He is wiser than us, and His plans are always good, regardless of what they may look like initially. His heart of love begins to touch, impact and then transform our heart, until the two hearts beat as one. This is a love walk with Jesus. As we grow closer to Him He will give us His vision and His perspective on things. Trust will grow and then He will begin to reveal His plans, His purposes and His love for others in your midst. He may start by highlighting a situation that He wants to release His love into. You may be called to buy lunch for someone, with what appears to be simple results. Later you might discover that your act of kindness helped save a marriage, brought encouragement or averted a suicide. You might be directed to show an act of kindness at your workplace or to the person in the cubical next to you or in line at the coffee shop. Small things first, and then as you learn to hear Him clearer, and trust grows on each side, He will send you into more exciting situations, with dramatic outcomes. He may direct you to approach someone you don't know and share a prophetic word, or lay hands on the sick for healing, or enter a hospital with a specific room number to release His Kingdom. As you grow and grow, one day you might find yourself standing before a multitude of people, proclaiming His Word. Walking with Jesus at times can be thrilling! At other times it can be challenging. It won't be without opposition. God uses both extremes to train you to hear His voice amidst all the other voices of the world. You'll grow from "faith to faith" (Romans 1:17), "strength to strength" (Psalms 84:7), and "glory to glory" (2 Corinthians 3:18). Hearing His voice on the journey to freedom is the best experience in the world. Throughout it all, as you continue to go deeper into His presence, you will find rest and peace for your soul.

Jesus said, "Take My yoke upon you and learn from Me, for I am gentle and humble in heart, and YOU WILL FIND REST FOR YOUR SOULS. "For My yoke is easy and My burden is light" (Matthew 11:28-30 KJV). God's burden is always light when we are walking in true agreement with him. He carries most of the load. However, when we aren't in agreement with him, and pull away from his yoke, the weight of the yoke becomes ours, and life becomes difficult, until we get back in agreement with Him.

God's highest will for your life is that you learn to hear His voice, because all the other voices in the world will fight against the plans and purposes that God has for you. Hearing His voice enables you to navigate the traps of the enemy and walk you safely to the other side where there is freedom. Now, let's identify and learn how to distinguish God's voice from all the other voices of the world. His Voice brings freedom. Let's take the next steps into your journey to freedom!

INTRODUCTION
SEVEN DIFFERENT KINDS OF VOICES

"There are, it may be, so many kinds of voices in the world, and none of them is without signification [significance]."
(1 Corinthians 14:10 KJV)

The word Voices in this passage is Strong's Concordance Greek Word **#5456 phóné**, pronounced, *Pho-nay*, and it means, 1) a Sound, 2) a Tone, 3) a Voice, 4) Speech.

When we think about the voice of God, we must understand God's voice includes a sound, a tone, a voice or speech. The Bible says that God spoke to Moses as a man speaks to his friend, "even face-to-face" (Numbers 12:8 NKJV). This means God spoke to Moses audibly. God speaks to people in various ways. God spoke to the prophets in "dreams and visions" (Numbers 12:6 NKJV). These had to seek Him and ask the interpretation of what He was communicating. He spoke to Elijah in the "still small voice" (1 Kings 19:12 KJV). Jesus spoke to the masses in parables. He also speaks "in songs of the night" (Job 35:10 NIV). Or "as we wake in the morning" (Psalms 143:8 KJV). Or "your ears will hear a voice behind you, saying, "This is the way; walk in it."" (Isaiah 30:21 NIV). **God speaks in various ways.** Section two of this book includes a topical guide to *Hearing God Speak in 25 Different Biblical Ways*. The full book is available in paperback or Kindle on *www.Amazon.com*. First, let's focus on the **Seven Different Kinds of Voices** in this world, beginning with **The Voice of God**. Then we will expose and dissect the other six kinds of voices that vie for our attention in this life. We will also learn how to recognize and avoid these when they are in conflict with the Master's Voice.

TABLE OF CONTENTS

Chapter 1: The Voice Of God 1
Chapter 2: The Voice Of Satan 6
Chapter 3: The Voice Of World 12
Chapter 4: Voice Of Flesh 17
Chapter 5: The Voice Of Soul... 25
Chapter 6: The Voice Of The Dead 33
Chapter 7: The Voice Of Religion 36
Chapter 8: The Hidden Voice - The Voice Of Blood 44
Chapter 9: Impartations And Spiritual Gifts 52
Chapter 10: The Power Of Praying In The Holy Spirit 60
Chapter 11: You Can Receive Gifts By Impartation From The Lord. 64
Chapter 12: People May Not Always Understand Or Agree With You
.... 73
Chapter 13: Climbing The Seven Cultural Mountains Of Influence .. 81
Conclusion 94

BONUS - SECTION 2 96

25 Ways God Speaks Today 96
Conclusion 120
7 Keys To Properly Hearing God 122
Final Prayer 126

CHAPTER 1
THE VOICE OF GOD

The Voice of God is recorded throughout the 66 books of the Bible, from Genesis to Revelation. God the Father speaks first from Heaven to create the earth (Genesis 1:1-3), God the Son speaks in his resurrected state to Saul of Tarsus on the road to Damascus (Acts 9:3-5), and God the Holy Spirit speaks to the Apostles to send others on ministry assignments for evangelism (Acts 13:2-3). *All three of these examples are equally the voice of God.* In addition, God's voice speaks through His Prophets, His angels, the Voice of Heaven, and in at least one place through the mouth of a donkey (Numbers 22:28-31)! All these accounts are God speaking through His yielded vessels and each should be recognized as God communicating to His children. "For everything that was written in the past was written to teach us, so that through the endurance taught in the Scriptures and the encouragement they provide we might have hope" (Romans 15:4 NIV). Let's start with an account of The Voice of the Father speaking from Heaven to those present during the baptism of Jesus.

  a) **Voice of the Father**—(Mark 1:11)—"And there came a **voice from heaven**, saying, Thou art my beloved Son, in whom I am well pleased." In this passage the Father's voice audibly endorses His Son before the people when Jesus is baptized in water and His ministry begins. As we will see later in this book, God the Father still speaks today.

Just before Jesus went to the Cross for our sins the Father speaks audibly again in response to Jesus' prayer, "Father, glorify thy name.

Then came there a voice from heaven, saying, I have both glorified it, and will glorify it again. The people therefore, that stood by, and heard it, said that it thundered: others said, An angel spake to him." (John 12:28-29 NKJV)

This is a stunning passage to me. If God the Father spoke audibly from heaven when you were present would you recognize it as God's voice? Most of the people present did not recognize this as the voice of God. Instead, those who stood thought "it thundered," or that "an angel spoke to Jesus" instead? How is this possible? I believe that when we are *leaning into God* we will learn to recognize His voice, when we are not pressing into God and not trying to hear Him, we could miss our day of his visitation upon our lives (Luke 19:44). We will discuss this in more detail later in this book as we learn to effectively recognize and obey God's voice rather than all the other voices of the world.

> b) **Voice of the Son**—(Acts 9:3-5)—"And as Saul journeyed, he came near Damascus: and suddenly there shined round about him a light from heaven: And he fell to the earth, and heard a voice saying unto him, Saul, Saul, why persecutest thou me? And he said, Who art thou, Lord? **And the Lord said, I am Jesus whom thou persecutest."**

In this passage Jesus appears after his resurrection from the dead. Jesus then speaks to a man named Saul of Tarsus, who is out murdering Christians while thinking he is doing God a service by killing them. Jesus sharply corrects him by knocking Saul to the ground and asking Saul audibly, 'Why are you persecuting me?" The result and fruit of Saul's encounter with the risen Savior speaking to him is repentance and salvation. Saul then learned to hear God's voice and became a mighty force for Jesus in the earth. Jesus still speaks today.

On another occasion Jesus appeared to two of his disciples in his resurrected form on the Road to Emmaus and taught them the Scriptures (Luke 24:14-25). What is interesting is even though these two disciples had walked with Jesus for three years, heard his voice and saw his miracles, in this situation they didn't recognize this was Jesus walking and talking with them until later. "When he was at the table with them, he took bread, gave thanks, broke it and began to give it to them. **Then their eyes were opened and they recognized him, and he disappeared from their sight.** They asked each other, "Were not our hearts burning within us while he talked with us on the road and opened the Scriptures to us?" (Luke 24:30-32 NIV).

The Bible says, "God, who at sundry times and in divers manners spoke in time past unto the fathers by the prophets, Hath in these last days spoken unto us by his Son, whom he hath appointed heir of all things, by whom also he made the worlds" (Hebrews 1:1-2 NKJV).

c) **Voice of the Spirit**—(1 Timothy 4:1)—"Now the Spirit speaketh expressly, that in the latter times some shall depart from the faith, giving heed to seducing spirits, and doctrines of devils." The Holy Spirit still speaks today.

John 16:13, NIV says, "But when he, the Spirit of truth, comes, he will guide you into all truth. He will not speak on his own; he will speak only what he hears, and he will tell you what is yet to come."

d) **Voice of the Holy Prophets**—(Luke 1:70)—"As he spoke by the mouth of his holy prophets, which have been since the world began."

The voice of the Holy Prophets is still active today inside men and women who are filled with the Holy Spirit. Phillip the Evangelist had four unmarried daughters who prophesied by the Holy Spirit (Acts 21:9). Scripture says that we "may all prophesy" (Acts 14:31). When you learn how to hear the Holy Spirit accurately He will trust you to prophesy; speaking forth His words and His heart to others. God's heart is a heart filled with love for His children.

e) **Voice of Heaven**—(Revelation 18:4) "And I heard another voice from heaven, saying, Come out of her, my people, that ye be not partakers of her sins, and that ye receive not of her plagues."

The voice of Heaven still speaks today. "Jesus is the same yesterday, today and forever" (Hebrews 13:8) and our Bible says, "I the Lord, change not" (Malachi 3:8). You can hear God's voice today, and as you read further, you will discover that He has already been speaking to you.

f) **Voice of Angels**— (Revelation 10:1-7) "And I saw another mighty angel come down from heaven, clothed with a cloud: and a rainbow was upon his head, and his face was as it were the sun, and his feet as pillars of fire: And he had in his hand a little book open: and he set his right foot upon the sea, and his left foot on the earth, **And cried with a loud voice, as when a lion roareth: and when he had cried, seven thunders uttered their voices. And when the seven thunders had uttered their voices,** I was about to write: and I heard a voice from heaven saying unto me, Seal up those things which the seven thunders uttered, and write them not. And the angel which I saw stand upon the sea and upon the earth lifted up his hand to heaven, And sware by him that liveth for ever and ever, who created heaven, and the things that therein are, and the earth, and the things that therein are, and the sea, and the things which are therein, that there should be time no longer: But in the days of the voice of the seventh angel, when he shall begin to sound, the mystery of God should be finished, as he hath declared to his servants the prophets." Here we have (1) the voice of a mighty angel, (2) the voice of the seven thunders, (3) the Voice of Heaven, and (4) the voice of the seventh angel. These all appear to speak to the servants the prophets, who will then proclaim the message to the people.

g) **The voice of an animal**— (Numbers 22:28-31) "**Then the LORD opened the donkey's mouth, and it said to Balaam,**

"What have I done to you to make you beat me these three times?" Balaam answered the donkey, "You have made a fool of me! If only I had a sword in my hand, I would kill you right now." **The donkey said to Balaam,** "Am I not your own donkey, which you have always ridden, to this day? Have I been in the habit of doing this to you?" "No," he said. Then the LORD opened Balaam's eyes, and he saw the angel of the LORD standing in the road with his sword drawn. So he bowed low and fell facedown."

This encounter demonstrates that God can speak through anyone, even a donkey, for His divine purposes. Jesus said if people remain silent that God will cause "even the rocks to cry out." (Luke 19:40). God is not limited, and as we will see in the next section, the devil can be quite creative in the ways he speaks through people as well.

CHAPTER 2
THE VOICE OF SATAN

(Demons, Lying Spirits, False Prophets, False Doctrines, Doctrines of Demons, Well-meaning voice of loved ones)

∞

The Bible story of mankind begins in the Garden of Eden with Adam and Eve. After Adam finished naming all the animals, God blessed him with a wife. It was then the devil showed up to upset their place of God's daily fellowship, peace and prosperity. Satan chose a serpent as his vessel to speak through in an effort to deceive these two King's kids out of their God-given inheritance.

Genesis 3:1-6: "Now **the serpent** was craftier than any of the wild animals the LORD God had made. **He said to the woman, "Did God really say,** 'You must not eat from any tree in the garden'?" The woman said to the serpent, "We may eat fruit from the trees in the garden, but God did say, 'You must not eat fruit from the tree that is in the middle of the garden, and you must not touch it, or you will die.'" "You will not surely die," **the serpent said to the woman.** "For God knows that when you eat of it your eyes will be opened, and you will be like God, knowing good and evil." When the woman saw that the fruit of the tree was good for food and pleasing to the eye, and also desirable for gaining wisdom, she took some and ate it. She also gave some to her husband, who was with her, and he ate it."

The enemy of our souls, Satan, still speaks today. He operates through his extensive army of demons, lying Spirits, false prophets and false teachers to introduce doctrines of Demons to deceive people out of their inheritances and destinies. Satan even speaks, at times, through the mouths of well-meaning friends, like those who gave Job poor quality advice during his time of trouble (Job chapters 31-34). Job's wife, during her time of grieving, loss and pain became Satan's emissary to speak words of suicide to the Prophet Job.

Let's look into Job's troubles. First Satan bargained with God for permission to inflict Job with sickness so that Job would be tempted to curse God to his face (Job 2:4-6).

"Satan replied. "A man will give all he has for his own life. But now stretch out your hand and strike his flesh and bones, **and he will surely curse you to your face."**

The LORD said to Satan, "Very well, then, he is in your hands; but you must spare his life."

Then Satan looked for a vessel he could get to Job through, someone close to him. He found an opening in the life of Job's wife during her time of grief.

Job 2:8-11: "Then Job took a piece of broken pottery and scraped himself with it as he sat among the ashes. **His wife said to him, "Are you still maintaining your integrity? Curse God and die!"** He replied, "You are talking like a foolish woman. Shall we accept good from God, and not trouble?" In all this, Job did not sin in what he said."

This is one of the ways in which the devil works today. Speaking to us through the mind, words and voices of our family, friends, coaches, boss, pastors or trusted advisors. To guard against this plot of the enemy we must become mature and properly recognize the enemy's voice in the midst of all the other voices of the world. God has our best interest in mind while the enemy seeks to derail us from fulfilling our destiny.

a) **Voice of Devils, Doctrines of Demons**—1 Timothy 4:1-3 "Now the Spirit speaketh expressly, that in the latter times some shall depart from the faith, giving heed to seducing spirits, and doctrines of devils; Speaking lies in hypocrisy; having their conscience seared with a hot iron; Forbidding to marry, and commanding to abstain from meats, which God hath created to be received with thanksgiving of them which believe and know the truth."

The Bible admonishes us to learn to recognize the voice of the enemy operating through seducing spirits and doctrines of devils. We are to recognize and reject these. The Bible is the infallible Word of God, meaning it is our rulebook and standard to recognize and then stand against these false doctrines.

Paul wrote this to the members of the Church of Galatia before he addressed the doctrines of legalism that had crept into their fellowship. Paul called it "another Gospel." This is an example of "doctrines of demons." Paul said these doctrines snared and brought these men and women of God into bondage after Christ had set them free (Galatians 5:1).

"I marvel that you are turning away so soon from Him who called you in the grace of Christ, to a different gospel, which is not another; but there are some who trouble you and want to pervert the gospel of Christ. But even if we, or an angel from heaven, preach any other gospel to you than what we have preached to you, let him be accursed. As we have said before, so now I say again, if anyone preaches any other gospel to you than what you have received, let him be accursed" (Galatians 1:6-9 NKJV).

We must "test the spirits" with the Word of God so we can stand in the liberty by which Christ has set us free. To accomplish this the Holy Spirit will give you insight and truth as you seek His counsel. He is well able to keep you from deception because He is the Spirit of Truth, and he will lead and guide you to stay on the right path. Jesus spoke these words regarding the Holy Spirit. I "will give you another Helper, to be with you forever, even the Spirit of truth, whom the world cannot receive, because it neither sees him nor knows him. You know him, for he dwells with you and will be in you" (John 14:16-17 NKJV). Because of this promise and empowerment from God you are never without Truth; Truth on the inside of you by the Holy Spirit and Truth from the Scriptures, "...because greater is he that is in you, than he that is in the world" (1 John 4:4 KJV).

b) Voice of False Prophets and False Ministers

The Bible has many warnings about False Prophets and False Ministers.

"For such are false apostles, deceitful workers, transforming themselves into the apostles of Christ. And no marvel; for Satan himself is transformed into an angel of light. Therefore it is no great thing if his ministers also be transformed as the ministers of righteousness; whose end shall be according to their works" (2 Corinthians 11:13-15).

To ensure we hear and obey the right voice it is important we spend time in the Scriptures daily and in prayer so we can properly "test the spirits" to determine if they are from God or the devil (1 John 4:4-6). We should also ask God for a Holy Spirit filled "accountability partner." Someone we can pray with and bounce things off of to ensure we are "in the faith." Regular practice of "testing the spirits," reading the Word and having an accountability partner who loves Jesus will enable us to effectively distinguish "the spirit of truth from the spirit of err" (see 1 John 4:6 KJV).

c) Voice of Demons, Spiritual Frogs, Dragon, Beast and the False Prophet—

"And I saw **three unclean spirits like frogs** come out of the **mouth of the dragon**, and out of **the mouth of the beast**, and out of the **mouth of the false prophet**. For they are the **spirits of devils**, working miracles, which go forth unto the kings of the earth and of the whole world, to gather them to the battle of that great day of God Almighty.

Behold, I come as a thief. Blessed is he that watches, and keeps his garments, lest he walk naked, and they see his shame" (Revelation 16:13-15).

The above are witchcraft spirits which run rampant in certain circles. (For a deeper dive into recognizing and defeating the spirit of witchcraft and demon spirits I recommend my book, *"Dealing with Demons"* available in paperback or Kindle on www.Amazon.com).

d) Voices of Lying Spirits

"And the LORD said unto him, Wherewith? And he said, I will go forth, and **I will be a lying spirit in the mouth of all his prophets.** And he said, Thou shalt persuade him, and prevail also: go forth, and do so. Now therefore, behold, the LORD hath put **a lying spirit in the mouth of all these thy prophets**, and the LORD hath spoken evil concerning thee" (1 Kings 22:22-23).

This is an unusual passage. Here God sends a lying spirit into the mouths of false prophets to entice a prideful and wicked king to his own death. To be fair, God also sends Micaiah, a righteous prophet to warn the King of the false prophets who are prophesying to the King. Moreover, God graciously tells the King exactly what is taking place. The King rejects the true prophecy and embraces the false. The Bible says, "And for this cause God shall send them strong delusion, that they should believe a lie:

That they all might be damned who believed not the truth, but had pleasure in unrighteousness" (2Thessalonians 2:11-12 NKJV).

The King loved unrighteousness and pride more than truth and God. The king rejects the true prophecy and God's prophet and strikes Micaiah in the mouth. He then imprisons Micaiah for speaking truth as God's voice on the earth. The King heads off into battle and dies. The Bible references such accounts and tells us, "These things happened to them as examples and were written down as warnings for us, on whom the culmination of the ages has come." (1Corinthians 10:11 NIV). We can either be God's role models, or a horrible warning for others, depending on what voice we listen to and obey. The choice is ours.

CHAPTER 3
THE VOICE OF WORLD

(Worldly Wisdom, Wisdom of Man, Worldly Ways, If it feels good, Do it!)

There are three types of wisdom in the Bible: (1) Worldly Wisdom, (2) Godly Wisdom, and (3) Man's Wisdom. Let's look at a passage on this from the Book of James:

"**Who *is* a wise man** and endued with knowledge among you? let him shew out of a good conversation his works with meekness of wisdom. But if ye have bitter envying and strife in your hearts, glory not, and lie not against the truth. **This wisdom descendeth not from above, but *is* earthly, sensual, devilish.** For where envying and strife *is*, there *is* confusion and every evil work. **But the wisdom that is from above** is first pure, then peaceable, gentle, *and* easy to be intreated, full of mercy and good fruits, without partiality, and without hypocrisy. And the fruit of righteousness is sown in peace of them that make peace" **(James 3:13-18 KJV).**

Worldly wisdom appeals to the senses and the emotions of mankind. In contrast, the wisdom that is from God reflects and reveals Jesus. Jesus is the wisdom of God. When we hear God speak and then follow the wisdom that flows from his voice, His character and nature becomes part of us and then shines through us. "But of him are ye in Christ Jesus, who of God is made unto us wisdom, and righteousness, and sanctification, and redemption:" (1Corinthians 1:30 KJV). Earthly wisdom tells us to follow our heart, which may sound like a good idea until we read God's warning in Jeremiah, which says "the heart is deceitful above all things" (Jeremiah 17:9). We each need a redeemed heart that only God can give us. The Bible says that God wants to take out our old stony heart and put a new heart from Him inside us.

"I will give you a new heart and put a new spirit in you; I will remove from you your heart of stone and give you a heart of flesh. And I will put my Spirit in you and move you to follow my decrees and be careful to keep my laws." (Ezekiel 36:25-27 NIV).

God will then move us from the inside and our actions will line up with the character of Jesus, who operates in love for others.

Worldly wisdom says seeing is believing, while godly wisdom from Jesus says, "Blessed are those who have not seen and yet have believed (John 20:29). Godly wisdom empowers us to "walk by faith, not by sight" (**2 Corinthians 5:7**). Earthly wisdom says love your family and friends, godly wisdom from above tells us to go one step further; "love your enemies and bless them" (Matthew 5:43-47). Earthly wisdom says there are many ways to God, godly wisdom tells us in Acts 4:12 there is only one way to God, Jesus Christ, and "there is no other name under heaven whereby men must be saved."

God's wisdom produces results. Jesus said, "Wisdom is justified by its children" (Matthew 11:19 KJV). Another translation reads, "But wisdom is proved right by her deeds" (NIV). The New Living translation says, "The Son of Man, on the other hand, feasts and drinks, and you say, 'He's a glutton and a drunkard, and a friend of tax collectors and other sinners!' But wisdom is shown to be right by its results." The litmus test is fruit. Jesus said, 'A tree is known by its fruit" (Matthew 7:15).

If the voice you're hearing is God's voice, it will be rooted in the Tree of Life. A good root will produce good fruit, and this fruit will remain. If the voice has a bad root, it will produce bad fruit, and comes from the Tree of the Knowledge of good and evil. In certain situations, only time can tell the real source, but the Holy Spirit will tell you clearly if you are trained to listen and discern. For Jeremiah he heard the voice of God instructing him to "buy a field," but wasn't sure if it was God speaking at first. Ten days later, Jeremiah received confirmation in the natural and then he knew this was the voice of God.

"Then Hanamel my uncle's son came to me in the court of the prison according to the word of the LORD, and said to me, 'Please buy my field that *is* in Anathoth, which *is* in the country of Benjamin; for the right of inheritance *is* yours, and the redemption yours; buy *it* for yourself.' Then I knew that this was the word of the LORD" (Jeremiah 32:8 NKJV).

We don't always know right away, but if we "wait upon the Lord" God will confirm it "by the mouth of two or three witnesses" (2Corinthians 13:1; Deuteronomy 19:15; Matthew 18:16).

Voices of Evil Men—"But evil men and seducers shall wax worse and worse, deceiving and being deceived" (2 Timothy 3:13 KJV). Evil men are known by their fruit. "By their fruit you will recognize them. Do people pick grapes from thornbushes, or figs from thistles? Likewise, every good tree bears good fruit, but a bad tree bears bad fruit" (Matthew 7:16-17 NIV). These evil men operate in a spirit and voice of deception. They operate in two primary categories with their words: 1) predators, and (2) parasites. The predator seeks to deceive someone out of something or take it from them or simply to destroy. The parasite latches onto its host and slowly, over time, sucks the life the person, while adding no real value. Empty words. These evil men operate in worldly wisdom, worldly ways and worldly counsel. They eat from the tree of the knowledge of good and evil that got Adam and Eve banished from the Garden of Eden. Beware of the voices of evil men, they are present in the marketplace, workplace and the church.

Before Paul died as Christ's martyr, he penned these poignant words from a prison cell about his preaching with God's power instead of just the enticing words of man's wisdom:

"And my speech and my preaching were not with enticing words of man's wisdom, **but in demonstration of the Spirit and of power:** That your faith should not stand in **the wisdom of men,** but in the power of God. Howbeit we speak wisdom among them that are perfect: yet **not the wisdom of this world,** nor of the princes of this world, that come to nothing: But **we speak the wisdom of God** in a mystery, even the hidden wisdom, which God ordained before the world unto our glory" (1 Corinthians 2:4-7 KJV).

James tells us the secret to receiving God's wisdom in abundance from Heaven:

"If any of you lacks wisdom, **you should ask God**, who gives generously to all without finding fault, and it will be given to you" (James 1:5). He goes on to state, "**But let him ask in faith**, with no doubting, for he who doubts is like a wave of the sea driven and tossed by the wind. For let not that man suppose that he will receive anything from the Lord; *he is* a double-minded man, unstable in all his ways.

The secret to receiving God's wisdom can be seen in three steps: (1) ask God for wisdom, and (2) believe by faith that you will receive it from him, and (3) then act upon what he shows or tells you to do.

I encourage you to take a moment right now and ask God for wisdom utilizing these three easy steps. Let's pray:

Heavenly Father, you said that if I ask for wisdom you will give it to me. Today by faith I ask for wisdom, and believe I receive it right now in the mighty name of your Son Jesus. Now, by faith, I step out and apply the wisdom you're speaking to me now and in the future regarding this and other matters you choose to reveal to me. Amen and amen.

Now you can fully expect Gods wisdom to be released to you in abundance, because you have asked. As situations arise in your life where you need wisdom, ask the Lord specifically for wisdom for the situation as you trust Him for each one. As Paul prayed for the Church members at Ephesus. I pray this prayer for you now.

That God "would grant you, according to the riches of His glory, to be strengthened with might through His Spirit in the inner man, that Christ may dwell in your hearts through faith; that you, being rooted and grounded in love, may be able to comprehend with all the saints what is the width and length and depth and height—to know the love of Christ which passes knowledge; that you may be filled with all the fullness of God" (Ephesians 3:16-20 NKJV).

And also, Paul's prayer for the Colossians:

"For this reason we also, since the day we heard it, do not cease to pray for you, and to ask that you may be filled with the knowledge of His will in all wisdom and spiritual understanding; that you may walk worthy of the Lord, fully pleasing Him, being fruitful in every good work and increasing in the knowledge of God; strengthened with all might, according to His glorious power, for all patience and longsuffering with joy; giving thanks to the Father who has qualified us to be partakers of the inheritance of the saints in the light. He has delivered us from the power of darkness and conveyed us into the kingdom of the Son of His love." (Colossians 1:9-13 NKJV).

I highly encourage you to pray these two above prayers from God's word often. Then watch and see what God begins to do and accomplish in and through your life as you learn to listen, hear and obey His voice as He speaks to and through you to the glory of Jesus.

CHAPTER 4
VOICE OF FLESH

(Lust of the Flesh, Voice of the Flesh, Self-Indulgence)

The voice of the flesh speaks loudly; when it's tired, hungry, selfish or just simply wants to be satisfied outside the timing and purposes of God. The Bible says, "For everything in the world-- the cravings of sinful man, the lust of his eyes and the boasting of what he has and does--**comes not from the Father but from the world**." **(1 John 2:16).**

Jesus was tempted in the wilderness during his forty days of fasting in the wilderness. His flesh must have spoken to him several times, "I'm hungry! How much longer before I can eat?" Satan used this opportunity of Jesus' weakened flesh to tempt him three distinct times (Matthew 4:1-11). Jesus leaned into God and overcame these **three temptations**. "**Therefore, submit to God. Resist the devil and he will flee from you**" (James 4:7 NKJV). In doing this, Jesus chose to obey the voice of God over the voice of his flesh and the enticing voice of Satan his enemy. Let's look at this temptation.

"Then Jesus was led up by the Spirit into the wilderness to be tempted by the devil. And when He had fasted forty days and forty nights, afterward He was hungry. Now when the tempter came to Him, he said, "If You are the Son of God, **command that these stones become bread**." But He answered and said, "It is written, 'Man shall not live by bread alone, but by every word that proceeds from the mouth of God.' " Then the devil took Him up into the holy city, set Him on the pinnacle of the temple, and said to Him, "**If You are the Son of God, throw Yourself down.** For it is written: 'He shall give His angels charge over you,' and, 'In *their* hands they shall bear you up, Lest you dash your foot against a stone.' " Jesus said to him, "It is written again, 'You shall not tempt the LORD your God.' " Again, the devil took Him up on an exceedingly high mountain and showed Him all the kingdoms of the world and their . he said to Him, "**All these things I will give You if You will fall down and worship me.**" Then Jesus said to him, "Away with you, Satan! For it is written, 'You shall worship the LORD your God, and Him only you shall serve.' " Then the devil left Him, and behold, angels came and ministered to Him." (Matthew 4:1-11).

These three **temptations** can be categorized as: (1) **hedonism** (hunger/satisfaction), (2) **egoism** (spectacular throw/might) and (3) **materialism** (kingdoms/wealth). The Bible refers to these three **temptation categories** as the (1) "lust of flesh" (hedonism), (2) "pride of life" (egoism) and (3) "lust of the eyes" (materialism).

Jesus overcame all <u>three</u> temptations. Let's find out how Jesus accomplished this and then follow his role-model in our own walk of victory and freedom with God.

1) Lust of the Flesh (hedonism)- "Now when the tempter came to Him, he said, "If You are the Son of God, command that these stones become bread."" (v. 3)

Jesus heard Satan's voice and then tested it against the Word of God; quoting the Book of Deuteronomy. "It is written, 'Man shall not live by bread alone, but by every word that proceeds from the mouth of God.' (v 4 - quoting from Deuteronomy 8:3).

Satan's verbal attack against Jesus failed when Jesus returned with the Word of God on the matter, silencing the voice of the enemy. Satan learned from his first round in the ring with Jesus. Satan immediately took a page out of Jesus' playbook in round two by quoting Scripture (out of context, of course) to Jesus in an effort to trick the Savior.

1) **Pride of Life (egoism)**– "If You are the Son of God, *throw Yourself down*. For it is written: 'He shall give His angels charge over you."

Jesus is not tricked by the devil's quotation of Scripture and responds with God's voice on the matter quoting Scripture, **"It is written again, 'You shall not tempt the LORD your God"** (v. 7 - quoting from Deuteronomy 6:16).

It is important to notice that Jesus quoted Scripture in proper context back to Satan to overcome his enemy's competing voice. Jesus wins the second round. But the enemy comes back a third time. This time Satan offers Jesus the kingdoms of the world. He speaks to Jesus' flesh and humanity. "Oh, look here Jesus, you don't have to endure the pain and suffering of the Cross in your body and die on the Cross. I'll just give you what you came for, the kingdoms of the world that Adam and Eve lost at the Tree of the Knowledge of good and evil. I'll give it all back to you right now. Here's a short cut, just bow down and worship me, and it's all yours." Let's look.

2) Lust of the Eyes (materialism). "And Satan said to Him, "All these things I will give You if You will fall down and worship me."

Jesus responds with a TKO against the enemy. He quotes the Word of God, God's written voice, trumping the voice of the Satan, ending the fight.

Then Jesus said to him, **"Away with you, Satan! For it is written, 'You shall worship the LORD your God, and Him only you shall serve.'"** (v. 7 - quoting from Deuteronomy 6:13).

Jesus has demonstrated how to win against the enemy. Prayer, fasting and spending time in the Word. This is the three-piece punch that knocks the enemy out every time.

If Jesus role-modeled study, fasting and quoting the Word of God audibly to silence the enemy's voice, then these are the unfailing keys to overcoming temptation on our freedom journey with Jesus. It is interesting to note that Jesus overcame the temptations of the flesh from the Book of Deuteronomy. When was the last time you read the Book of Deuteronomy? This might be a good weapon to have in your arsenal.

Adam and Eve in the Garden

In the Garden of Eden these same three strike points were triggered by Satan in front of the Tree of the Knowledge of Good and evil.

"Now the serpent was more cunning than any beast of the field which the LORD God had made. And he said to the woman, "Has God indeed said, 'You shall not eat of every tree of the garden'?" And the woman said to the serpent, "We may eat the fruit of the trees of the garden; but of the fruit of the tree which *is* in the midst of the garden, God has said, 'You shall not eat it, nor shall you touch it, lest you die.'"

"Then the serpent said to the woman, "You will not surely die. For God knows that in the day you eat of it your eyes will be opened, and you will be like God, knowing good and evil." So when the woman saw that the tree *was* **good for food,** that it *was* **pleasant to the eyes,** and a tree **desirable to make *one* wise**, she took of its fruit and ate. She also gave to her husband with her, and he ate" (Genesis 3:1-6 NKJV).

Adam and Eve failed this tri-fold temptation. Both Adam and Eve willingly made the decision to eat from this forbidden fruit. Notice how their senses were triggered in all three areas:

"So when the woman saw that the tree *was* **good for food,** that it *was* **pleasant to the eyes,** and a tree **desirable to make *one* wise**, she took of its fruit and ate. She also gave to her husband with her, and he ate" (v. 6).

All three temptations that Jesus overcame in the wilderness Adam and Even fell prey to in the Garden. The Tree of the knowledge of good and evil offered fruit that was: 1) "good for food" (lust of the flesh), (2) "pleasant to the eyes" (lust of the eyes), and "desirable to make one wise" (pride of life). When these two lovebirds ate to satisfy these three areas of their flesh, they stepped onto the trading floors of the enemy. They traded the temporary fleshly benefits for their perfect Garden of Eden. Everything changed that day. They lost their dominion. They spiritually died. They lost fellowship with God. They knew they were naked. They began to toil and make a living by the sweat of their brow. The good news is Jesus won our dominion back at the Cross and has given everything back to us that Adam lost. The future is bright!

We all battle the flesh

During our time on earth, we each battle three common temptations; (1) the lust of the eyes, (2) the lust of the flesh, and (3) the pride of life. This battle continues from the day we are born until the day we die. Even the apostle Paul said he had to "die daily" to the old nature of the flesh, the Adamic nature we are all born into this world with. "I affirm, by the boasting in you which I have in Christ Jesus our Lord, I die daily" (1Corinthians 15:31 NKJV). King David said, " Behold, I was shapen in iniquity; and in sin did my mother conceive me" (Psalms 51:5 kJV).

God calls us to "crucify the old nature", this is a daily, and sometimes minute by minute action. One person said, 'The problem with a living sacrifice is it keeps crawling off the altar." We must guard against these fleshly voices and "take every thought captive unto the obedience of Christ" (2 Corinthians 10:5). The Apostle Paul identified various voices that speak to us from our flesh. He identified **at least 17 works of the flesh** by name. He begins this presentation by saying, "The works of the flesh are evident" (Galatians 5:16 NKJV). Let's examine these:

The Works of the Flesh

"The acts of the flesh are obvious: sexual immorality, impurity and debauchery; idolatry and witchcraft; hatred, discord, jealousy, fits of rage, selfish ambition, dissensions, factions and envy; drunkenness, orgies, and the like. I warn you, as I did before, that those who live like this will not inherit the kingdom of God" (Galatians 5:17-21, NIV).

Paul says, 'Those who live like this will not inherit the kingdom of God." Strong words. It's imperative that we recognize these self-evident works of the flesh speaking to us from the old dead nature. Paul goes on to contrast these fleshly works with God's desire for us to bear "the fruit of the Holy Spirit" in and through our lives. He names nine of these spiritual fruits that come from God.

"But the fruit of the Spirit is love, joy, peace, patience, kindness, goodness, faithfulness, gentleness, self-control; against such things there is no law. Now those who belong to Christ Jesus have crucified the flesh with its passions and desires" (Galatians 5:22-23 NIV).

Recognizing the voice of the flesh and their earmark signs speaking to us enables us to speak back to it with the Word of God and trump it every time, bringing these competing voices to silence. "We demolish arguments and every pretension that sets itself up against the knowledge of God, and we take captive every thought to make it obedient to Christ" (2 Corinthians 10:5 NIV).

When we rely on the gift of the Holy Spirit, our helper, our teacher, our comforter that Jesus gave us, He will quicken us to God's Word in the situation. He will bring into remembrance all things that He's spoken to us during our study time in the Bible. Then we have spiritual arrows that fell the enemy by the words out of our mouth under the anointing of the Holy Spirit. We will overcome temptation every time with the greater voice of God. We have been given the ability, in the power of the Holy Spirit, to win every battle the enemy throws at us! God always makes a way for us to overcome or escape the tempting voices of the enemy triggering our flesh. Let's look at God's promise on this matter.

"No temptation has overtaken you except what is common to mankind. And God is faithful; he will not let you be tempted beyond what you can bear. But when you are tempted, he will also provide a way out so that you can endure it" (1Corinthians 10:13 NIV).

Jesus our Role-Model

As we see in these above examples, Jesus role-modeled the proper way to overcome every competing voice from our flesh. Jesus knew the key to unlock heaven into the situation was to only say and do what He saw and heard the Father speaking to him. "Then Jesus answered and said to them, "Most assuredly, I say to you, the Son can do nothing of Himself, but what He sees the Father do; for whatever He does, the Son also does in like manner." (John 5:19-20 NKJV).

If you ask God to give you "eyes to see" and "ears to hear" then He will do it for you. Take a moment and ask Him now.

Father, I pray for you to give me spiritual eyes to see and ears to hear what the Spirit is saying to me in this very hour. Tune my ears to hear the frequency of Heaven. I want to hear your voice. I don't want to hear you speak and think it thundered, but I want to know your voice above all the other voices of the world. I ask this humbly and boldly now in the name of your Son, Jesus Christ.

The Battle Victory is Yours

The battle victory is yours. To walk in full victory, it's important to know that God never sends temptation to you, but He will allow temptation from these other voices, including the voice of your flesh, to speak to you. He allowed this with Jesus, but the Father never tempted Jesus, the devil is the tempter. During these times you can recognize this as a test. You are in God's classroom of life, and he has equipped you to pass every test in advance. Let's not skip out on the classroom instruction from the Lord so we know what to answer when the tests come. Once you pass the test God will reward you. He will promote and give you more authority.

"When tempted, no one should say, "God is tempting me." For God cannot be tempted by evil, nor does he tempt anyone; but each person is tempted when they are dragged away by their own evil desire and enticed. Then, after desire has conceived, it gives birth to sin; and sin, when it is full-grown, gives birth to death." (James 1:13-14 NIV).

As we can see, the choice is ultimately yours in which voice you listen to and act on. Choose today to be be a child of God who hears His voice like Jesus and God will always be faithful to empower you to overcome. God honors your desire to obey Him. When you honor God with the desire to obey Him, He will empower you to overcome. Remember, when temptation comes, and it will come, God promises to always make a way of escape if we will only look for it. Today you've been empowered with this knowledge. Next time temptation comes, look for the escape route and take it to victory! Next let's look at another voice that competes with God's voice, the voice of your soul.

CHAPTER 5
THE VOICE OF SOUL

(The Redeemed Soul and The Unredeemed Soul)

This is a lifetime process that comes with repeated rewards for every temptation we overcome. Each one begins with saying yes to the voice of God over the voices of the world.

"Therefore, I urge you, brothers, in view of God's mercy, **to offer your bodies as living sacrifices, holy and pleasing to God--** this is your spiritual act of worship. **Do not conform any longer to the pattern of this world, but be transformed by the renewing of your mind.** Then you will be able to test and approve what God's will is-- his good, pleasing and perfect will" (Romans 12:1-2).

We have three primary weapons in this battle.

We have three primary weapons in this battle against the accuser, the devil and his team of competing voices. These three weapons are: (1) the Word of our Testimony, (2) the Blood of the Lamb, and (3) loving Jesus more than ourselves. Let's look at these.

"Then I heard a loud voice saying in heaven, "Now salvation, and strength, and the kingdom of our God, and the power of His Christ have come, for the accuser of our brethren, who accused them before our God day and night, has been cast down. And they overcame him by the **blood of the Lamb** and **by the word of their testimony**, and they did not love their lives to the death." (Revelation 12:9-10 NKJV).

Jesus said, "If anyone comes to Me and does not hate ("love less") his father and mother, wife and children, brothers and sisters, yes, and his own life also, he cannot be My disciple" (Luke 14:26 NKJV).

We must love God more than anyone or anything else. This includes our own lives; our desires, goals, dreams, aspirations, partner choice, career, etc. This may sound hard, but the beauty is that once we love God more than any of these people or things, God's love will fill us and enable us to love them even more.

Jesus also said, "Greater love has no one than this, than to lay down one's life for his friends" (John 15:13 NKJV).

These are bookends in God's love for us and mankind. If we love Him first and foremost, He will enable us to love others to the utmost!

Honoring God with our bodies

When we honor God with our body instead of yielding our flesh to the other voices of the world, our ability to hear God's voice and will becomes sharper and keener When we fall prey to temptation and yield our bodies to the lust of the flesh, the lust of the eyes or the pride of life, our hearing becomes dulled. The more we yield to God the easier it becomes, the more we yield to the other voices, the more difficult it becomes to accurately distinguish God's voice from the others. Our hearing becomes dull. Some have obeyed the voice of the enemy and their flesh for so long that their conscience becomes seared like with a hot iron. "Now the Spirit expressly says that in latter times some will depart from the faith, giving heed to deceiving spirits and doctrines of demons, speaking lies in hypocrisy, **having their own conscience seared with a hot iron**" (1 Timothy 4:1-2 KJV).

Once a conscience is "seared"—literally "cauterized"—then it becomes insensitive. Such a conscience does not work properly; it's as if "spiritual scar tissue" has dulled the sense of right and wrong. Just as the hide of an animal scarred with a branding iron becomes numb to feeling further pain, so the heart of an individual with a seared conscience becomes desensitized to God's voice convicting them of right and wrong. We can repent, ask God to forgive us, cleanse our mind and heal our soul. He will respond. This act on our part resets the coordinates on our spiritual journey, like a GPS recalculates with a U-turn and places us back on the right track with God.

Some characteristics of the voice of an unredeemed soul (a man's mind, will and emotions) speaking with himself is below:

"**And I will say to my soul**, Soul, thou hast much goods laid up for many years; take thine ease, eat, drink, *and* be merry." But God said to him, 'Fool! This night your soul will be required of you; then whose will those things be which you have provided?. **(Luke 12:19-20 KJV)** The New International Version reads, "**And I'll say to myself,** "You have plenty of grain laid up for many years. Take life easy; eat, drink and be merry"'" (V. 19).

Jesus warned, "For what shall it profit a man, if he shall gain the whole world, and lose his own soul? Or what shall a man give in exchange for his soul? **(Mark 8:36-37 KJV).**

The unredeemed soul thinks of its own pleasure or what will benefit itself, or cause decisions to be made out of emotions. Such as anger, fear, jealousy, and hatred that can cause wrong decisions to be made.

The Redeemed Soul (the mind, will and emotions of Christ)

We can get to a place where our soul is redeemed and truly loves and honors God. When this occurs we hear the voice of our redeemed soul and it is the voice of God that has filled us with His Word. The redeemed soul, the part that has been transformed by the renewing of our minds, is the mind of Christ speaking to us. We become sealed in that area of our thinking.

"And you shall love the LORD your God with all your heart and with all your soul and with all your might" (**Deuteronomy 6:5 KJV**).

We all go through a process to get to this place. God allows certain things to come up at different times in our journey to mature us into the mind of Christ in this area of our soul. The Bible even talks about times when we are in "bitterness in soul" during our prayer time. When we cry out from this place of pain in our soul God answers and heals us in this bitter area. The bitterness then becomes sweet to our soul like honey. "How sweet are Your words to my taste, *Sweeter* than honey to my mouth!" (Psalms 109:3 NKJV).

This is part of what occurs when we are transformed by the renewing of our minds during prayer time, worship, fasting and reading God's Word (Romans 12:2).

"And Hannah *was* **in bitterness of soul**, and prayed unto the LORD, and wept sore." It's often during these painful times we make a vow to the Lord and the greatest response from Heaven comes. "Then she made a vow and said, "O LORD of hosts, if You will indeed look on the affliction of Your maidservant and remember me, and not forget Your maidservant, but will give Your maidservant a male child, then I will give him to the LORD all the days of his life, and no razor shall come upon his head."

God answered her prayer and turned her bitterness of soul into a sweet place, like honey. Hannah then miraculously conceived and gave birth to Samuel later that same year. Samuel grew up to learn to hear the Lord's voice. He would later become a great Prophet to all of Israel" (**1 Samuel 1:10-13 KJV**).

God would then train up this young child Samuel to hear the Master's voice. God did this so he could speak through a mature Samuel to give direction and victory to the nation of Israel. The first, second and third time God spoke to Samuel, he didn't know it was God speaking to him. This should encourage us on two fronts: (1) we may not always know when God is speaking to us, and (2) God is persistent and speaks again, and again until we recognize His voice.

"The LORD called Samuel; and he said, "Here I am." Then he ran to Eli and said, "Here I am, for you called me." But he said, "I did not call, lie down again." So he went and lay down. The LORD called yet again, "Samuel!" So Samuel arose and went to Eli and said, "Here I am, for you called me." But he answered, "I did not call, my son, lie down again." Now Samuel did not yet know the LORD, nor had the word of the LORD yet been revealed to him. So the LORD called Samuel again for the third time. And he arose and went to Eli and said, "Here I am, for you called me." Then Eli discerned that the LORD was calling the boy. And Eli said to Samuel, "Go lie down, and it shall be if He calls you, that you shall say, 'Speak, LORD, for Your servant is listening.'" So Samuel went and lay down in his place.

God then came a 4th time to Samuel.

"Then the LORD came and stood and called as at other times, "Samuel! Samuel!" And Samuel said, "Speak, for Your servant is listening" (1Samuel 3:5-10).

This time Samuel finally recognized this as the Voice of God speaking, and responded by saying, "Speak, for Your servant is listening" (vs 10).

The Lord then said to Samuel, "Behold, I am about to do a thing in Israel at which both ears of everyone who hears it will tingle. "In that day I will carry out against Eli all that I have spoken concerning his house, from beginning to end" (1Samuel 3:11-12 NIV).

Samuel learned to hear the voice of the Lord and was accurate in all that he spoke all the days of his ministry.

"The LORD was with Samuel as he grew up, and he let none of Samuel's words fall to the ground" (1Samuel 3:19 NIV).

God wants to give us this same testimony, to learn to hear His voice, speak for Him and release His love, power, goodness, healing and provision to his people in the earth. The apostle Peter confirmed this when he wrote by the Holy Spirit,

"As each one has received a *special* gift, employ it in serving one another as good stewards of the manifold grace of God. **Whoever speaks, *is to do so* as one who is speaking the utterances of God;** whoever serves *is to do so* as one who is serving by the strength which God supplies; so that in all things God may be glorified through Jesus Christ, to whom belongs the glory and dominion forever and ever. Amen." (1 Peter 4:10-11)

When challenges come, we must encourage ourselves in the Lord

When challenges come, these might bring us great distress. In moments when no one else is willing to encourage us, we must choose to encourage ourselves in the Lord. Remember, Jesus is always interceding for us before the throne of grace, 24/7 (Hebrews 7:24-25). If we turn to Him, we will find strength. Even though our trusted friends and comrades might turn away from us, or at times, may even turn against us, we have one who listens to our prayers and intervenes in our behalf.

David's 600 fighting men spoke of stoning him to death. How could they turn against their faithful leader? His men's souls were grieved because of a great loss. Their wives and children and possessions had been taken by the enemy. Instead of encouraging themselves in the Lord, they listened to the voice of the enemy, and wanted to kill their leader.

"And David was greatly distressed; for the people spake of stoning him, **because the soul of all the people was grieved**, every man for his sons and for his daughters…" (1Samuel 30:6a KJV).

King David role modeled how to "encourage himself in the Lord." David could have given up as their leader, but instead, the Bible says. **"but David encouraged himself in the LORD his God"** (1 Samuel 30:6b KJV).

At times we must decide to reach up to God for encouragement. We must quiet our souls so we can hear His voice above all the other voices clamoring for our attention. If we don't encourage ourselves in the Lord, there's no guarantee that anyone else will. This is a time of testing. If we pass these tests, we will be promoted. David became King after this. But in the moment no one was promoting David to King because of his leadership. He'd lost it all; including his own wives, children and possessions. They were all in the same boat together. Instead of discussing their community problem with David and then having a prayer meeting to seek God's counsel, they just wanted to stone him. It's said that if you want to be popular, don't be a leader, sell ice cream instead. True leadership will require you to hear God accurately, even when others around you don't agree with you. David pressed into God during the noise of all these voices, including the ones that threatened his life. David prayed and then God spoke the strategy of Heaven.

"So David inquired of the LORD, saying, "Shall I pursue this troop? Shall I overtake them?" And He answered him, "**Pursue, for you shall surely overtake *them* and without fail recover *all*"** (1Samuel 30:8 NKJV).

David told the men what God had spoken. They listened, agreed and followed the plan. God honored their obedience and empowered them to recover everyone and everything that was taken.

"So David recovered all that the Amalekites had carried away, and David rescued his two wives. And nothing of theirs was lacking, either small or great, sons or daughters, spoil or anything which they had taken from them; David recovered all" (1Samuel 3:18-19 NKJV).

None of us is perfect, we are all learning to hear God more clearly throughout our lives. When our emotions are strongest, such as with fear and anger it is sometimes more difficult to hear the Lord correctly. I encourage you in such times to quiet your inner storm so you can hear, get confirmation from Godly friends and wait on the Lord, do not quickly be led by strong emotions. This is one of the hardest times to hear, so do not be discouraged if you miss it and hear incorrectly, keep seeking God's voice and over time with practice we all get more accurate hearing in the midst of emotional situations.

CHAPTER 6
THE VOICE OF THE DEAD

(Necromancy, Old Nature)

Necromancy is strictly forbidden in the Scriptures. What is Necromancy?

Necromancy definition- The practice of magic involving **communication with the dead** – either by summoning their spirit as an apparition or raising them bodily – for the purpose of divination, imparting the means to foretell future events, discover hidden knowledge, or to use the dead as a weapon."

The Bible forbids communicating with the dead. This is a form of witchcraft. Let's look.

"When thou art come into the land which the LORD thy God giveth thee, **thou shalt not learn to do after the abominations of those nations**. There shall not be found among you anyone…that useth divination…or a witch…or a consulter with familiar spirits, or a wizard, **or a necromancer" (Deuteronomy 18:10-11 KJV).**

A prime example of the consequences of Necromancy is illustrated in the life of King Saul when he violated this necromancy prohibition and consulted a witch to communicate with the dead.

"Saul then said to his attendants, **"Find me a woman who is a medium, so I may go and inquire of her."** "There is one in Endor," they said. So Saul disguised himself, putting on other clothes, and at night he and two men went to the woman. "Consult a spirit for me," he said, "and bring up for me the one I name." But the woman said to him, "Surely you know what Saul has done. He has cut off the **mediums and spiritists** from the land. Why have you set a trap for my life to bring about my death?" Saul swore to her by the LORD, "As surely as the LORD lives, you will not be punished for this." Then the woman asked, "Whom shall I bring up for you?" **"Bring up Samuel,"** he said. When the woman saw Samuel, she cried out at the top of her voice and said to Saul, "Why have you deceived me? You are Saul!" The king said to her, "Don't be afraid. What do you see?" The woman said, "I see a spirit coming up out of the ground." "What does he look like?" he asked. "An old man wearing a robe is coming up," she said. Then Saul knew it was Samuel, and he bowed down and prostrated himself with his face to the ground. Samuel said to Saul, "Why have you disturbed me by bringing me up?" "I am in great distress," Saul said. "The Philistines are fighting against me, and God has turned away from me. He no longer answers me, either by prophets or by dreams. So I have called on you to tell me what to do." Samuel said, **"Why do you consult me,** now that the LORD has turned away from you and become your enemy? The LORD has done what he predicted through me. The LORD has torn the kingdom out of your hands and given it to one of your neighbors-- to David" Because thou obeyedst not the voice of the LORD, nor executedst his fierce wrath upon Amalek, therefore hath the LORD done this thing unto thee this day. Moreover the LORD will also deliver Israel with thee into the hand of the Philistines: and tomorrow shalt thou and thy sons be with me: **(1 Samuel 28:7-18 KJV).**

Saul departed from necromancy-based encounter with Samuel through the Witch of Endor, and then went into battle against his enemies. Saul didn't even try to seek the Lord or repent asking God for mercy. Saul listened to the voice of his own prideful soul; resulting in the deaths of his sons, and then Saul committed suicide by falling on his own sword. David became King in his place.

"And the battle went sore against Saul, and the archers hit him; and he was sore wounded of the archers" Then said Saul unto his armourbearer, Draw thy sword, and thrust me through therewith; lest these uncircumcised come and thrust me through, and abuse me. But his armourbearer would not; for he was sore afraid. **Therefore, Saul took a sword, and fell upon it**" (1Samuel 31:3-4 KJV).

The voice of your dead flesh—This voice speaks to us daily. Paul told us "to put to death" our old nature. Let's look

"**Put to death, therefore, whatever belongs to your earthly nature**: sexual immorality, impurity, lust, evil desires and greed, which is idolatry. Because of these, the wrath of God is coming. You used to walk in these ways, in the life you once lived. But now you must also rid yourselves of all such things as these: anger, rage, malice, slander, and filthy language from your lips. Do not lie to each other, since you have taken off your old self with its practices and have put on the new self, which is being renewed in knowledge in the image of its Creator" (Colossians 3:5-11 NIV).

Many Christians operate in a form of necromancy with their old earthly nature. The nature of Adam speaks to them and they respond. They entertain these thoughts, even speak back to these words, entertaining them. King David made this mistake after he became King. He listened to the voice of his flesh and went after Bathsheba. This cost the lives of 70,000 people by plague. Necromancing with our old dead nature, instead of crucifying it, can be expensive. Not worth the price. Silence the voice with Word of God. Say, "I am dead to sin, but alive with God in Christ Jesus" (Romans 6:11 KJV).

Stay away from the voice of the dead. Don't necromance. Especially with the voice of your old dead nature that was crucified with Christ. The final voice is the deadliest of them all…

CHAPTER 7
THE VOICE OF RELIGION

(Pharisees, Sadducees, Religious Rules and Regulations that oppose True Relationship with God, and His Word).

The **voice of religion is probably the most dangerous and diabolical voice of them all.** This is the same manipulative voice that swayed God's people to accept the murder of Jesus. This voice operated unhindered through the Pharisees and Sadducees who used religious words to direct both the religious and political narrative of the day. The voice of religion swayed the masses of God's people under their spiritual authority. This voice moved the people to shout, "Crucify him, crucify him!" (Luke 34:21 KJV). The political leader of the time didn't want to crucify Jesus. Pontus Pilate sought to release Jesus because he knew Jesus had done no wrong. Jesus hadn't broken any of the Roman laws, he hadn't caused any problems with the authorities, but the religious spirit hated him and was out for blood! "From then on, Pilate tried to set Jesus free, but the Jewish leaders kept shouting, **"If you let this man go, you are no friend of Caesar. **Anyone who claims to be a king opposes Caesar.""** Simply put, the religious spirit worked with the political spirit to crucify Jesus. When the political spirit declined crucifixion of an innocent man, the religious spirit shouted in a manner of speaking, "Pilate, it's either you or Jesus, you decide! If you choose Jesus, we will tell Cesar on you!"

Simply put, **the voice of religion is a murdering spirit.** Jesus said the Pharisees, who knew the Bible backwards and forward, said they were sons of Satan. He told them they were just like their father the devil, who was a murderer and liar (see John 8:43-45). Strong words!

The Political Spirit vs the Religious Spirit

The political spirit washes its hands of you when you are no longer of use to it. The religious spirit seeks to kill you. Let's look.

Political Spirit – Pontus Pilate: "When Pilate saw that he was getting nowhere, but that instead an uproar was starting, he took water and washed his hands in front of the crowd. "I am innocent of this man's blood," he said. "It is your responsibility!" (Matthew 27:24 NIV).

Religious Spirit – Pharisees and Sadducees: All the people answered, "His blood is on us and on our children!" (Matthew 27:25 NIV).

The Political Spirit and the Religious Spirit work together to accomplish a common purpose. In the case of Jesus, the political spirit reluctantly worked with the religious spirit to remove Jesus from the scene in Jerusalem. Usually these two spirits oppose each other, meaning they are at odds. For example, the religious leaders hated the Roman government. But when the religious leaders lacked authority to crucify Jesus, they turned to Pilate, who had political authority, to accomplish their murderous act. The religious spirit wanted Jesus crucified so the people would no longer follow him. Jesus was upsetting their religious business model. Jesus confronted called their hypocrisy, calling them "blind guides" (Matthew 15:14). He also said,

"Woe to you, teachers of the law and Pharisees, you hypocrites! You are like whitewashed tombs, which look beautiful on the outside but on the inside are full of the bones of the dead and everything unclean. In the same way, on the outside you appear to people as righteous but on the inside you are full of hypocrisy and wickedness" (Matthew 23:27-28 NIV).

Jesus' actions, love and miracle working power upset the religious leaders. They couldn't compete with this. Under Jesus' authority and leadership, the people were taught and shown God's love; these people were healed, delivered, set free, their blind eyes opened, deaf ears unstopped, lepers cleansed, lame walked, they experienced instant forgiveness of sin and even received their children back from the dead (Matthew 11:5).

Under the Pharisees' and Sadducees' authority and leadership the people received only judgment, condemnation and shame. The religious voice offered only rules and regulations in addition to the 613 Levitical laws through Moses. The voice of religion added to the word of God and the religious leaders then created thousands of additional rules that kept the people in further religious bondage. They offered no answers or enablement to the people that would empower them to overcome sin. The religious voice spoke to tell people what they were not, and how each of them failed the law and deserved only death. Jesus, in contrast, came to set the people free from the law and introduce them to grace. This would be accomplished through the ultimate voice that would speak on their behalf after the resurrection!

There is an ancient proverb that says, **"The enemy of my enemy is my friend."** This proverb suggests that two opposing parties can or should work together against a common enemy. This was the case with political Pilate, the religious Pharisees and Saducees and their common enemy, Jesus, the voice of God on the earth. They sought to silence the voice of God.

The religious voice preaches and teaches the letter of the law that only brings death to our souls. Jesus taught the Spirit of the Word that brings life to our souls. The Pharisees wanted to stone a woman caught in adultery. They wanted her dead! The religious voice is a murdering spirit! No mercy. Jesus on the other hand, forgave her and told her, "I do not condemn you, either. Go. From now on sin no more." (John 8:11 NASB). The love of God delivers us from sin. The letter of the law condemns us in our sin, with no hope of redemption. Paul the Apostle, a former Pharisee, was using his "letter of the law voice of religion" to kill Christians thinking he was doing God a service before he was converted. "Meanwhile, Saul was uttering threats with every breath and was eager to kill the Lord's followers. So, he went to the high priest" (Acts 9:1 NLT). Saul, who later became Paul after his Damascus road conversion, had a murdering spirit; this is the real motive behind the voice of religion. It's no different today.

He went from law to grace. God "rescued us from the dominion of darkness and brought us into the kingdom of the Son he loves" (Colossians 1:13 NIV).

When Paul met Jesus on the road to Damascus God changed his heart. He then penned these words, God "has made us competent as ministers of a new covenant--not of the letter but of the Spirit; **for the letter kills, but the Spirit gives life**. (2 Corinthians 3:6 NIV).

Jesus echoed this sentiment during his life on earth. In recognizing the voice of religion Jesus told the Pharisees that they "made the commandment of God of none effect **by their tradition" (Matthew 15:6 KJV).** We must guard against exalting our traditions above what God is doing in the moment. God told Moses to create a bronze serpent and lift it up on a pole. "All who looked on the serpent were healed" (See Numbers 21:9). This is what God was doing in the moment, and it resulted in healing. "Those who are led by the Spirit are sons of God" (Romans 8:14). Years later God told King Hezekiah to destroy this same bronze serpent because it had become an idol in the eyes of God's people; the Israelites had begun burning incense to it as a [false] god (2 Kings 18:4 KJV). They took their eyes off God, the source, who told them to look upon the serpent and God would heal them. They put their eyes on the serpent and forgot God as their source and supply. This wrong focus on the serpent instead of the one who created it, came back to bite them! This is exactly what the voice of religion's goal is, to distract our eyes away from Jesus and redirect our eyes on anything other than Jesus. This includes religious rules and regulations, our church attendance, amount of time we spend in prayer or Bible study, or evangelism outreaches, or our ability to fast long periods of time, or any of our own self-willed works of righteousness. Anything that supplants the work of Jesus accomplished at the Cross on our behalf and his empowerment of the Holy Spirit to accomplish our assignment in the earth is an affront to Jesus and our relationship with God. **This voice of religion has turned more people away from God than all the other voices combined.**

Paul was well acquainted with the voice of dead religion. He wielded the power of worldly wisdom and used it effectively to verbally manipulate the scriptures and cause the death of many of Jesus' disciples.

"And Saul, yet breathing out threatenings and slaughter against the disciples of the Lord, went unto the high priest, And desired of him letters to Damascus to the synagogues, that if he found any of this way, whether they were men or women, he might bring them bound unto Jerusalem. (Acts 9:1-2)

Paul used his Pharisaical authority to imprison and murder Christians. Jesus told Ananias just after Paul's conversion experience, "For I will shew him how great things he must suffer for my name's sake" (Acts 9:16 KJV). Later Paul, after folllowing Jesus for a few years and preaching the Gospel with signs and wonders following, then experienced persecution, imprisonment and eventually death at the hands of those still listening to and under the same influence of the voice of religion. **The voice of religion is a murdering spirit.** The voice of religion confuses and dulls people's senses from hearing, understanding or believing the truth. "The god of this world has blinded the minds of those who don't believe. They can't see the light of the good news that makes Christ's glory clear. Christ is the likeness of God" (2Corinthians 4:4 NIVR).

Jesus told the Pharisees, "Why do you not understand My speech? **Because you are not able to listen to My word. You are of *your* father the devil,** and the desires of your father you want to do" (John 8:43 NKJV).

Jesus goes on to say, "He [the devil] was a murderer, and does not stand in the truth, **because there is no truth in him**. When he speaks a lie, he speaks from his own *resources,* for he is a liar and the father of it. But because I tell the truth, you do not believe Me" (v. 44-45). These are strong words Jesus spoke about the religious leaders of the day; the Pharisees and Sadducees. Jesus said they were murderers and just like their father the devil, who is a perpetual liar.

Traditions vs. Traditionalism

"Thus, have ye made the commandment of God of none effect by your tradition" (Matthew 15:6 KJV)

There is a distinct difference between godly **traditions** handed down to us by our faith-filled fathers and mothers, and the **traditionalism of men** that is only religious in nature. Jesus said regarding the voice of religion and religious leaders, "They tie up heavy, cumbersome loads and put them on other people's shoulders, but they themselves are not willing to lift a finger to move them" (Matthew 23:4 NIV). One way we could illustrate this is to say, "Traditions are the *living faith* handed down to us by those who have since died, while traditionalism is the *dead faith* of those still living."

The Spirit of the Word vs. the letter of the law. Paul distinguished "living faith" that was handed down to his spiritual son Timothy by his grandmother and mother by role-model. He wrote to Timothy, "When I call to remembrance **the genuine faith that is in you**, which dwelt first in your grandmother Lois and your mother Eunice, and **I am persuaded is in you also.** Therefore I remind you to **stir up the gift of God** which is in you through the laying on of my hands" (2 Timothy 2:4-6 KJV).

Genuine faith is role-modeled and demonstrated in love through others. This type of faith can also be experienced and received during prayer times alone with the Lord. This can also occur through the "laying on of hands" by other anointed men and women of God. Paul said, "I long to see you that I might impart unto you some spiritual gift that at the end you might be established" (Romans 1:11 KJV). This type of spiritual impartation helps strengthen and establish us in the faith.

Jesus never judged by what he saw or heard in the natural. Solomon said that "Every argument sounds good until you hear the other side" (Proverbs 18:17).

The Old Testament prophet Isaiah foretells of the Messiah's wisdom, understanding, counsel, might, power, knowledge, and the fear of the Lord. Isaiah says that when he appears on the scene, he be endued with the Seven-fold spirit of God.

"The Spirit of the LORD shall rest upon Him,

The Spirit of wisdom and understanding,

The Spirit of counsel and might,

The Spirit of knowledge and of the fear of the LORD.

His delight *is* in the fear of the LORD,

And He shall not judge by the sight of His eyes,

Nor decide by the hearing of His ears;

But with righteousness He shall judge the poor,

And decide with equity for the meek of the earth" (Isaiah 11:2-4 NKJV).

The Seven-Fold Spirit of God is recorded above. Jesus is our role-model. He declared we could do the same type of works as Him by the gift of the Holy Spirit. Therefore, this same seven-fold empowerment is available for us today, if we ask Him.

1) Spirit of the Lord, 2) Spirit of Wisdom, 3) Spirit of Understanding, 4) Spirit of Counsel, 5) Spirit of Strength, 6) Spirit of Knowledge and 7) the Spirit of the Fear of the Lord.

Even as God is one but has three distinct personhoods: Father, Son and Holy Spirit. Likewise, the Holy Spirit is One but with seven distinct expressions. Do you want the fullness of the Holy Spirit operating in, upon and through your life? Let's ask God for this now.

Prayer for the Seven-Fold Spirit of God

Heavenly Father, I humbly yet boldly ask for the empowerment of the Seven-fold Spirit of God for my life, walk, business, family, ministry and career. I ask You to enable me to walk in and embody these seven characteristics in every situation I encounter. I believe this is a gifting that You want to empower me with. I also ask You to reveal to me how to flow in sync with the Holy Spirit in this gifting for Your people and for Your Glory. In Jesus Mighty Name I pray. Amen.

CHAPTER 8
THE HIDDEN VOICE - THE VOICE OF BLOOD

8). Voice of Blood – (The Blood of Abel and the Blood of Jesus).

∽∾

The voice of blood can speak against you, or for you. Both types of shed blood require an act or action on our part before they can speak. Let's look at two passages, one is the Blood of Abel, the other, the Blood of Jesus.

In the Book of Genesis, the blood of Abel spoke from the earth against his brother Cain, who had murdered him. Cain activated Abel's voice through murder! Cain's anger was fueled by religious jealousy.

Did you know that blood has a voice? According to the Bible it does.

And God said to Cain, "What have you done? **Listen! Your brother's blood cries out to me from the ground" (Genesis 4:10 NIV).**

God heard the voice of Abel's innocent blood crying up from the ground after his Brother Cain murdered him. God then made Cain accountable for his sin· "Now you are under a curse and driven from the ground, which opened its mouth to receive your brother's blood from your hand. When you work the ground, it will no longer yield its crops for you. You will be a restless wanderer on the earth" (Genesis 4:11-12 NIV).

This account of the first murder indicates those slain innocently have a voice that cries up to God, even though they are dead, their blood still speaks! Many people are murdered around the world every day, and their blood cries out. How many innocent babies who were murdered in the womb are dead, but their blood still speaks from the grave, crying up from the ground. Statistically, since 1973 in America alone we've had 50 Million abortions. This shocking number is like the number of lives lost in the 1st and 2nd world wars. The blood of these innocents cries up to God. Even though they are dead, their blood still has a voice and speaks on their behalf.

THE GOOD NEWS

There is good news. The Blood of the crucified Jesus also cries up to God, not against us, but on our behalf. Each time we sin and then repent by confessing our mistakes to God, He forgives us and applies the blood of Jesus that cries out on our behalf and instantly cleanses us from the stain of this sin. The Bible says that Jesus intercedes for us all day and all night, each day. We have an advocate with the Father, who is there to plead our case, 24/7. Let's look.

"And to **Jesus** the mediator of the new covenant, **and to the blood of sprinkling, that speaketh better things than that of Abel**" (Hebrews 12:24 KJV).

Jesus' blood is the final authority. **The voice of Jesus' blood silences every other voice of accusation.** Therefore, Jesus is able to save anyone who comes to God by Him. The author of Hebrews says it this way:

"But Jesus, on the other hand, because He continues forever, holds His priesthood permanently. Therefore He is able also to save forever those who draw near to God through Him, since He always lives to make intercession for them" (Hebrews 7:24-25 NIV).

Did you know that the blood of Jesus is always at work to cleanse you from sin? How encouraging! Did you know we also have a responsibility on our side to activate this cleansing blood's power? How you might ask? We simply bring our sin into the light for the blood to take action and cleanse us.

"This is the message which we have heard from Him and declare to you, that God is light and in Him is no darkness at all. If we say that we have fellowship with Him, and walk in darkness, we lie and do not practice the truth. **But if we walk in the light as He is in the light,** we have fellowship with one another, **and the blood of Jesus Christ His Son cleanses us from all sin" (1John 1:5-7 NKJV).**

Notice this passage says, **"If we walk in the light…the blood of Jesus Christ His Son cleanses us from all sin."** Jesus is always at work interceding for us before the throne of grace. We are on earth and are always invited to "confess our sins" and when we do, the blood of Jesus will cleanse us from all unrighteousness. Let's read on.

"If we say that we have no sin, we deceive ourselves, and the truth is not in us. **If we confess our sins, He is faithful and just to forgive us *our* sins and to cleanse us from all unrighteousness**. If we say that we have not sinned, we make Him a liar, and His word is not in us" **(1John 1:8:10 NKJV).**

The Blood of Jesus – Cleanses us from all sin. Have you applied the blood today? Have you brought your issues into the light with God? Do you want to be free?

If not, allow me to share this verse of direction to help move you closer to the Cross.

"How much more severely do you think someone deserves to be punished who has trampled the Son of God underfoot, **who has treated as an unholy thing the blood of the covenant that sanctified them**, and who has insulted the Spirit of grace?" **(Hebrews 10:29 NIV).**

Let's pray...

Father, I confess my sins to You. I acknowledge that I've had issues that I'm unable to fully overcome; besetting sins that I've struggled with, confessed to You on more than one occasion, You've forgiven me of, and then I stumble in the same area or trip over repeatedly. Today I ask for full deliverance once and for all. I fully confess and break ties with the sin of _____ and _____. I choose to obey Your voice above all the other voices of the world. Jesus, I ask You to deliver me from the generational iniquity cord that has bound me. I ask You to pull it out. Straighten the crooked nature I was born with from Adam that is inside my being. Empower me to grow straight and serve You with a pure heart. Take out any stony areas of my heart that remain and put Your heart of love within me for others. Move me to walk in Your ways and keep Your commands by the power of the Holy Spirit directing me from the inside. I ask this humbly and boldly now in Jesus mighty Name. Now I ask the blood of Jesus to fully speak for me and cleanse and purify me with the all forgiving, all powerful shed blood of Jesus. By faith I hear the words spoken by the blood that says I am "not guilty" in Jesus Name! Amen and Amen.

Take a moment to receive and rest in the presence of God descending up on your life. Allow him to restore your soul. He has cast your sin into the sea of forgetfulness; he remembers it no more. Moreover, he put up a sign that reads, "No fishing!" Glory to God.

Now take part in and enjoy his love, joy and refreshing from his tangible presence.

Prayer for forgiveness from all judgments

"Therefore, since we are receiving a kingdom that cannot be shaken, let us be thankful, and so worship God acceptably with reverence and awe, for our "God is a consuming fire." (Hebrews 12:22-28 **NIV).**

God wants to burn up every voice in your life that exalts itself against the knowledge of God. He wants to consume you in the fire of His presence. He wants to cause His Word to become like a fire shut up in your bones. To accomplish this we must forgive others any wrongs they have committed against us. This will free us from wrongdoing or judgments we have made against others.

God wants you to be free from all judgments; judgments you have made against others, judgments others have made against you, and judgments you have made against yourself, both knowingly and unknowingly. God declares you not guilty. His voice is the voice we must agree with and then the enemy loses all legal authority in our lives. When you pray this prayer something supernatural is going to shift on the inside of you and on the outside of you. The enemy is going to lose legal right against you and God's angels are going to come minister to you. Heaven is going to unleash blessings upon your life, house, business, relationships, and ministry. As you pray this prayer you may feel something lift off you, or leave your mind, body or soul.

The Bible is clear about holding grudges or unforgiveness against other people. Jesus said, "

"And whenever you stand praying, if you have anything against anyone, forgive him, that your Father in heaven may also forgive you your trespasses. But if you do not forgive, neither will your Father in heaven forgive your trespasses" (Mark 11:25-26 NKJV).

One of the reasons the enemy maintains a foothold in our lives is based on our own unforgiveness. Jesus tells us, "But if you do not forgive, neither will your Father in heaven forgive your trespasses" (v 26). Unforgiveness is like drinking poison in hopes that someone else will get sick from it. It doesn't work and only harms us. It's time to get free. The key to unlock the shackles of shame and the handcuffs of hatred is in your hand. Let's look at a parable that Jesus highlighted for us about this important issue on our journey to freedom.

"Then Peter came to Him and said, "Lord, how often shall my brother sin against me, and I forgive him? Up to seven times?" Jesus said to him, "I do not say to you, up to seven times, but up to seventy times seven" (Matthew 18:21-22 NKJV).

Jesus told Peter to forgive seventy-seven times; this number seven is the number for completion. Seventy-seven is the number that indicates Jesus wants us to forgive repeatedly, until everything is complete in our lives.

Jesus goes on to speak a parable about the Kingdom of Heaven.

"Therefore, the kingdom of heaven is like a certain king who wanted to settle accounts with his servants. [24] And when he had begun to settle accounts, one was brought to him who owed him ten thousand talents. [25] But as he was not able to pay, his master commanded that he be sold, with his wife and children and all that he had, and that payment be made. [26] The servant therefore fell down before him, saying, 'Master, have patience with me, and I will pay you all.' [27] Then the master of that servant was moved with compassion, released him, and forgave him the debt. [28] "But that servant went out and found one of his fellow servants who owed him a hundred denarii; and he laid hands on him and took *him* by the throat, saying, 'Pay me what you owe!' [29] So his fellow servant fell down at his feet and begged him, saying, 'Have patience with me, and I will pay you all.' [30] And he would not, but went and threw him into prison till he should pay the debt. [31] So when his fellow servants saw what had been done, they were very grieved, and came and told their master all that had been done. [32] Then his master, after he had called him, said to him, **'You wicked servant! I forgave you all that debt because you begged me. [33] Should you not also have had compassion on your fellow servant, just as I had pity on you?'** [34] And his master was angry, and delivered him to the torturers until he should pay all that was due to him.[35] "**So My heavenly Father also will do to you if each of you, from his heart, does not forgive his brother his trespasses."** (Matthew 18:22-35)

When we receive mercy, we should in like manner demonstrate mercy to others. If we don't give mercy that we received from God to others, allowing this act of kindness to flow through us, it will reverse the opposite direction on us. The Bible says God will punish us by sending the voice of tormenters into our life. Let's read on.

"And his lord was wroth, **and delivered him to the tormentors**, till he should pay all that was due unto him. So likewise shall my heavenly Father do also unto you, if ye from your hearts forgive not everyone his brother their trespasses." (Matthew 18:33-35 KJV).

To be free from the voices and afflictions of the tormentors, which can include tormenting spirits and demonic voices, **Jesus requires us to forgive**. Jesus forgave all his enemies while dying on the Cross for mankind's sins. He cried out, "Father, forgive them, for they do not know what they are doing" (Luke 23:34 NIV). Stephen followed this same role-model when he was being stoned to death for his faith. "Then Stephen fell on his knees and cried out, "Lord, do not hold this sin against them." When he had said this, he fell asleep" (Acts 7:60 NIV). When we forgive our enemies, it opens the door for their salvation. Remember, it was Saul of Tarsus that was standing by holding the religious people's coats as they murdered innocent Stephen who had been preaching Jesus. God confirmed His words with healings, miracles, deliverance from demons, signs and wonders that liberated God's people from dead dry religion. "And Stephen, full of grace and power, was performing great wonders and signs among the people" (Acts 6:8 NIV). The religious voice operating through the Pharisee, Saul of Tarsus, moved the people to murder.

"Saul was in hearty agreement with putting Stephen to death" (Acts 8:1). But because Stephen forgave from his heart, God did a post-mortem miracle in Stephen's ministry.

Jesus meets Saul of Tarsus on the road to Damascus and radically changes Saul through a face-to-face conversion experience. Saul becomes Paul and goes on to write two thirds of the New Testament. This is the power, wisdom and love of God in operation through forgiveness. When we forgive others Satan and his tormentors lose their legal right to torment us any longer and it opens the door for heaven to send Jesus into our enemy's life. Do you want this kind of power and freedom? If so, let's pray.

Prayer for release from Judging

Heavenly Father, I repent of all my sins. I forgive everyone, including myself from my heart. I repent from judging anyone, including myself, from my heart. I now command every spirit that's not of Jesus Christ to go quickly and quietly from my mind, will, imagination, body and soul and spirit. Jesus, I ask you to take any and all fractured parts in my soul and reintegrate these into wholeness and soundness now. I ask you for the mind of Christ. Holy Spirit I ask you to fill me with your presence and your power, permeating and taking over these vacant areas that are now open to you, in Jesus Mighty Name. Amen and Amen.

Now, take a moment to take a deep breath in and out a few times. Breath out the old and breath in the new, the Holy Spirit will fill you. Then take time to thank Jesus for forgiving you and delivering you from all tormentors once and for all and for filling you with His presence.

CHAPTER 9
IMPARTATIONS AND SPIRITUAL GIFTS

The apostle Paul knew the importance of impartation. He also knew how to impart spiritual gifts to strengthen people in their faith. He told the Church at Rome, "**I long to see you so that I may impart to you some spiritual gift to make you strong-**" (Romans 1:11 NIV). He told the Church at Corinth, "For in Christ you have been enriched in every way—with all kinds of speech and with all knowledge—God thus confirming our testimony about Christ among you. **Therefore you do not lack any spiritual gift** as you eagerly wait for our Lord Jesus Christ to be revealed" (1Corinthians 1:6-7).

Paul believed in impartation of spiritual gifts. The Holy Spirit recorded this in Scripture for a reason. We should seek God for impartations of spiritual gifts.

The Holy Spirit wrote through Paul's pen these poignant words to the Corinthians,

"Now concerning spiritual gifts, brethren, I would not have you ignorant" (1Corinthians 12:1 KJV). Then Paul went on to write three chapters about spiritual gifts, love and the operation of these gifts by love (see 1Corinthians chapters 12-14).

Impartations and spiritual gifts come in a variety of ways.

Impartations and spiritual gifts come in a variety of ways. You can receive spiritual gifts through the laying on of hands. A gift could come during a time of prayer or alone with God. God may even impart a gift to you in a dream while you sleep. He may send a gift with an angel to visit you while you are awake or asleep. A gift could be deposited into you during a word of prophecy through someone God sends across your path or in a church service. God is not limited. You may also receive a spiritual gift while reading the Bible and the verse simply jumps off the page and into your spirit, and bam, the gift is suddenly inside you. Gifts are just that, gifts. You don't do anything for them, or they would be rewards. These gifts are actually for others, through you. The gifts of healings, the gift of prophecy, the gift of tongues and interpretation of tongues, word of wisdom, word of knowledge, the working of miracles, the gift of faith, and so many more. God gives gifts to help establish you in the faith and to bless, deliver and empower his people through your vessel.

Once we receive impartations or gifts it becomes our choice to "stir up this gift" or "gifts" we received. I have been the recipient of various impartations through prayer and the laying on of hands in the above-mentioned ways. I have also received gifts during a dream. I woke up and the gifts deposited in me immediately began operating. No one taught me, it just happened. The Holy Spirit activated these gifts in me. He then set up divine appointments immediately after with other people for these gifts to operate through me. The gifts were for the people, they came through me immediately after these came to me. Word of Knowledge and Word of Wisdom. They were baby gifts to start with, and they grew stronger and stronger, with sharper clarity, greater detail and cleaner accuracy, as I was faithful to step out on faith and exercise these. God calls us to prophesy according to the proportion of our faith.

"We have different gifts, according to the grace given to each of us. If your gift is prophesying, then prophesy in accordance with your faith" (Romans 12:6 NIV).

Our faith increases over time as we go from faith to faith. Our gifts of healing may start with the anointing to heal a headache. As we exercise our faith the gifts of healing may be strong enough to heal brain cancer. We grow in grace.

Each one of these gifts or giftings that God imparted to me, and that you can also receive, was imparted or deposited in me in what I call a seed-form. Once in me, God causes it to increase in faith until it grows into a full-grown tree to "bear much fruit" and "fruit that remains." We receive the gifts by grace, and then steward these accordingly. God requires us to allow Him to develop, cultivate and nurture these gifts into maturity. If this is something you want from the Lord; to be utilized as one of His vessels to release His gifts and gifting to others, you will be required to nurture and "stir up the gifts." This takes time and occurs when you pray in the Holy Spirit, spend time in the Word, Praise, Worship and fellowship with Jesus and other like-minded believers. When we are faithful to exercise these biblical disciplines, our faith increases and soars until it is like a "fire shut up your bones." As a result, evangelism, healing, deliverance, and miracles flow to those God brings across your path. The operation of these gifts become almost effortless and occur organically by divine appointment. It is the Holy Spirit who orchestrates and directs the whole process.

In retrospect I now realize the gift or gifts of the Holy Spirit increased in strength, authority and power over time. I can now also see clearly that when I didn't take time to stir up the gift, the faith and fire imparted inside me from the Lord remained at a low ember level and produced little to no results. Like a car with no fuel. Praying in the Holy Spirit helps refill your tank with the anointing. This choice is always ours. I have learned over the last 30 years of my walk with Jesus that the gifts of the Holy Spirit are always moving, we're just not always in the Spirit to move in them. Therefore, we must "stir up the gift" and "fan the flame" and step into the moving of the Holy Spirit.

Jude, the author of a powerful single-chapter epistle, said these words, "But ye, beloved, **building up yourselves on your most holy**

faith, praying in the Holy Ghost," (Jude 1:20 KJV). Praying in the Holy Spirit, at times, will include praying in tongues.

Tongues for personal edification is given by Jesus through the Holy Spirit to empower a believer to strengthen his own spirit. The word "edification" means "to be a housebuilder," or "to build up, embolden or edify" (Strong's #3618–oikodomeo). When preaching about spiritual warfare and the armor of God, Paul began with these words, "Be strong in the Lord and the power of His might" (Ephesians 6:10). Tongues for personal edification (and spiritual strengthening) is a wonderful gift from God to His Church. Jude alludes to this gift near the end of his epistle. "But you, dear friends, must build up your lives ever more strongly upon the foundation of our holy faith, learning to pray in the power and strength of the Holy Spirit." (Jude 20, LVB). The word for "building up yourselves" is "epoikodomeo" (Strong's #2026) and comes from the same word Paul uses in 1Corinthians 14:4 when referring to tongues for personal edification (Strong's #3618–oikodomeo).

"Pray Without Ceasing"

The Apostle Paul, who the Holy Spirit directed to teach extensively on the different uses of tongues, declared, **"I thank my God that I speak in tongues more than all of you"** (1Corinthians 14:18), and also said, **"Pray without ceasing"** (1Thessalonians 5:17). Have you ever tried to pray "without ceasing" for even a few hours? It's difficult. I usually run out of words in English after only a half an hour or so. It's when I run out of words in English (things I know I need to pray about) that I then use my personal prayer language in tongues (things beyond my intellect and knowledge that the Holy Spirit knows about) to effectively pray through every line of the enemy's defense. This is when prayer takes on a whole new power, and breakthrough occurs. Prayers are answered in unusual and demonstrative ways.

Paul experienced the same prayer weakness you and I experience during his walk with Christ. We are all weak without the empowerment of the Holy Spirit, or worse, religious in our thinking and the other voices we listen to. In the natural, we are all limited, like a cell phone battery, limited in its charge. But God, by His Spirit, is unlimited, like the lightning from Heaven. We need our cell phone recharged and supercharged by heaven's unlimited resources and power. Therefore I believe Paul wrote to the Church at Rome these words:

"In the same way, **the Spirit helps us in our weakness**. We do not know what we ought to pray for, but the Spirit himself intercedes for us with groans that words cannot express" (Romans 8:26, NIV).

We need the empowerment of the Holy Spirit and every spiritual gift we can to help us effectively navigate through life.

Therefore, building yourself can be accomplished by praying in the Holy Spirit (Jude 1:20); or praying in private use tongues given by the Spirit for personal building (edification) (1Corinthians 14:3-4).

Is it Right for Me to Edify Myself?

A good question was recently asked when the subject of tongues came up. The person then quoted 1 Corinthians 14:4 "He who speaks in a tongue edifies himself". They asked, "Isn't it more important to edify others than edifying ourselves? Legitimate question, but I quickly recognized the wrong voice speaking. This is the religious voice of false humility. Let me give you an example. On an airplane they instruct you to put on your air mask first, and then help the person next to you. Otherwise you might not have enough air in your lungs to help others in trouble. The same is true about self-edification, breathing in the presence and empowerment of God. The scriptures are clear on this issue, and this is the voice that trumps all the other voices. **Paul commands us to edify ourselves in several places,** both directly and by example.

Paul's prayer for the Ephesians included these words, "that out of his glorious, unlimited resources He will give you the mighty inner strengthening of his Holy Spirit" (Ephesians 3:16, LVB). How does God grant us this supernatural inner strengthening? One of the ways this occurs is by exercising the God-given ability to pray in the Holy Spirit.

Since we have already addressed the above two direct passages (Jude 1:20; Ephesians 6:10), let's look to an example from King David's life in the Old Testament. David had just been attacked at Ziglag by the Amalekites and lost everything. His wives were taken captive and the city had been burned (1 Samuel 30:12). His band of 600 soldiers was very upset about this. They lost everything too. They wanted to stone David (1 Samuel 30:6). David was discouraged, to say the least. But, instead of giving up and throwing in the towel, the Bible says, "...but David encouraged himself in the Lord his God" (vs. 6, KJV). The Hebrew word for "encouraged himself" is "chazaq" (Strong's # 2388). It means "to strengthen one's self," much like the Greek word used in 1 Corinthians 14:4 "to edify or build up oneself." In fact, the term was also frequently used for construction (as in Matthew 7:24, 26). It's important to strengthen, encourage and build ourselves up in the Lord, praying in the Holy Spirit privately. Then we are strong in the Lord and the power of His might to go and edify, strengthen and encourage others.

You can ask for the Gift of Praying in Other Tongues

Every Believer in Jesus can ask for the gift of praying in other tongues. This is your personal prayer language between you and God. He will give you this gift.

This gift is another tool from God to strengthen your spirit and build you up. This will empower you to minister in power to others. Praying in tongues privately gives you power to preach the gospel publicly. Praying in tongues privately releases heaven's will into situations you don't even know about, but God does. This is the reason I encourage people to pray in tongues as often as they can throughout the day. "Pray without ceasing" (1 Thessalonians 5:17).

Your prayer language in tongues for personal edification is different from the gift of speaking in tongues for public use. (If you want to learn more about how to distinguish between these two types of speaking in tongues, I recommend you read my book on this powerful subject. "What the Bible REALLY says about speaking in Tongues", available in paperback and Kindle, Amazon.com). This book will also teach you about the Four Different Types of Tongues God makes available to empower you. These are 1.) **tongues as a sign to the unbeliever** (1 Corinthians 14:22), 2.) **tongues for personal edification** (1 Corinthians. 14:4), 3.) **tongues for interpretation** (1 Corinthians 14:5) and 4**.) tongues for deep intercessional groanings** (Romans 8:26). **If you want this gift, you can ask God right now.** Your life will never be the same.

Let's pray for God to give you the infilling of the Holy Spirit with the prayer language of tongues now, and any additional types of tongues He wants to activate in you at this time.

Prayer for Holy Spirit Infilling and Power

Dear Heavenly Father, I thank You for the gifts You have given to Your children. I now have a better understanding of the gift of tongues and earnestly desire to receive this gift into my life. I repent for speaking against this gift knowingly or unknowingly. I ask and receive in faith knowing that even as I pray that You are setting the wheels in motion to manifest this gift in my life. I thank You for the gift of tongues that will deepen my relationship with You and Your Beloved Son, Jesus Christ. I thank You that through this gift, I will be personally built up and will also edify and build up the church, Your Body. Thank you that I will have that supernatural convincing power of the Holy Spirit as I witness to the lost souls of this world. Give me wisdom and discernment in the exercise of this gift, that it may only bring greater glory to You. I ask all this in Jesus' Mighty Name. Amen.

Now that you've prayed this simple prayer trust God to honor his promise to fill you with His Holy Spirit. Begin to thank and praise him for giving you this gift with the outward evidence of speaking in other tongues. Say, "Lord, I thank you by faith for giving me this gift so I can honor you, build up my own spirit by praying in tongues daily, and be able to strengthen and build up others. By faith, I believe I have received and fully expect to speak in other tongues by the Holy Spirit." Now as an act of faith begin to praise and thank God until the Holy Spirit wells up within your spirit and bubbles forth with words in another language; a language you have never spoken before. It may be somewhat strange to you at first because it is supernatural in nature. Just open your mouth like you will talk but do not use your known language, and Holy Spirit will give you words. It is the Holy Spirit giving you these words, His words, to glorify the Father. Trust Him and yield to the Holy Spirit. Spend a few minutes now yielding to the Holy Spirit and praising God, trusting Him to do the rest.

CHAPTER 10
THE POWER OF PRAYING IN THE HOLY SPIRIT

When we pray in the Holy Spirit it causes us to be built up with supernatural power on the inside. We get charged up, so to speak. Once we are fully charged, we are positioned to release Heaven's power into situations on the outside of us. One example of this is the Apostle Peter. He was so built up on the inside from prayer time with God that people recognized he carried something. In response, they brought their sick and afflicted and demon tormented and lined these people up in the streets so that Peter's shadow might touch them. And they were all healed! Let's look.

"So that they brought the sick out into the streets and laid *them* on beds and couches, **that at least the shadow of Peter passing by might fall on some of them.** Also a multitude gathered from the surrounding cities to Jerusalem, bringing sick people and those who were tormented by unclean spirits, **and they were all healed**" (Acts 5:15-17 NKJV).

The apostle Paul spend hours and hours in prayer. He learned what it meant to "pray without ceasing" (1Thessalonians 5:17). Paul learned how to hear God's voice above all the other voices in the world by spending time alone with the Master. He obeyed the voice of the Holy Spirit and then experienced supernatural results in all that he put his hand to do. He walked in agreement with Jesus by the power and wisdom of the Holy Spirit.

Do you want this kind of power? Now that you've prayed the prayer for the fresh power of the Holy Spirit you can have it too. Jesus promised and now wants you represent Him in the earth. What does this mean? To represent something is to "re-present" it. Jesus did the works of the Father, and if we "re-present" Jesus we will see the same types of works. Jesus said that because He is sending the Holy Spirit to us that we could do "even greater works" (John 14:12-14 KJV). It begins each day by spending time alone with God so we can effectively get the marching orders for the day. During these quiet times of fellowship, He will often speak or show you something that will occur later that day. And then it will. You will say and do what the Father has already shown you earlier, just like Jesus demonstrated for us (John 5:19-20).

The Apostle Paul spent hours and hours praying in tongues. In fact, he said, "I thank my God I speak with tongues more than you all" (1Corinthians 14:18 NKJV). Paul prayed in tongues privately and during these times of prayer he experienced revelation, interpretation, fellowship with God and a fully built up spirit on the inside. He echoed the words of Jude when he said, "**He who speaks in a tongue edifies himself**" (1Corinthians 14:4 NKJV). Paul was "edifying himself" or "building himself up" on the inside during these times of prayer, so he could walk in God's wisdom, strength, healing power and miracles in the church, highways and wherever God sent him during his life. Paul was so anointed from these prayer times with the Lord that even the clothing on his body was saturated with God's healing and delivering power.

"Now God worked unusual miracles by the hands of Paul, so that even handkerchiefs or aprons were brought from his body to the sick, and the diseases left them, and the evil spirits went out of them" (Acts 19:11-12 NKJV).

Paul, the man who claimed to pray in tongues more than anyone, said these words,

"For I will not dare to speak of any of those things which Christ has not accomplished through me, in word and deed, to make the Gentiles obedient—in mighty signs and wonders, by the power of the Spirit of God, so that from Jerusalem and round about to Illyricum **I have fully preached the gospel of Christ**" (Romans 15:18-19 NKJV).

To **fully preach the Gospel of Christ** we must have God's power. Anything less results in only an intellectual message with limited results. We must have his authority in our voice, words and deeds. We must have the power that changes lives and converts souls. We must have Holy Spirit boldness that comes by spending time with Jesus and is imparted to us from Heaven.

"**And when they had prayed**, the place where they were assembled together was shaken; and they were all filled with the Holy Spirit, **and they spoke the word of God with boldness**" (Acts 4:30-31 NKJV)

Paul knew the difference between intellectual words and true power. He had been a Pharisee. By age seven he had memorized the first five books of the Bible. As a Pharisee he could quote the entire Old Testament from memory. But he lacked the power of Heaven in his life. In fact, he operated in the power of the law, and imprisoned and murdered people who preached God's love and power in Christ. He had been listening to the wrong voice, the voice of Religion. But then he heard a second voice on the road to Damascus. It was the voice of Jesus, who wanted a relationship with him. Paul accepted this Jesus and learned to hear His voice above all the other voices of the world. The more time He spent in the presence of Jesus the more Christlike Paul became. Instead of boasting in his knowledge, he boasted that he knew Jesus and walked in the power of His resurrection. Then he penned these words:

"But then "And I, brethren, when I came to you, did not come with excellence of speech or of wisdom declaring to you the testimony of God. For I determined not to know anything among you except Jesus

Christ and Him crucified. I was with you in weakness, in fear, and in much trembling. **And my speech and my preaching *were* not with persuasive words of human wisdom, but in demonstration of the Spirit and of power, that your faith should not be in the wisdom of men but in the power of God"** (1Corinthians 2:1-5 NKJV).

Paul prayed in tongues privately and had power publicly. He also received revelation during these extended times of prayer. These times of revelation enabled him to write two thirds of the New Testament.

"But I make known to you, brethren, that the gospel which was preached by me is not according to man. [12] For I neither received it from man, nor was I taught *it,* **but *it came* through the revelation of Jesus Christ"** (Galatians 1:11-13 NKJV).

CHAPTER 11
YOU CAN RECEIVE GIFTS BY IMPARTATION FROM THE LORD

You can receive gifts by impartation from the Lord. God wants to give you His gifts during your times of prayer and fasting. He does this so He can release these gifts to others through you. He wants to touch, bless, encourage, heal, and empower others in the earth. To accomplish this, He may also impart gifts to you through men or women of God by "the laying on of hands." Once you receive a spiritual gift or gifts, you can then develop these gifts deposited into you over time and they will grow. Whether prophecy, healing, sign gifts, the power to cast out devils, writing music, art, business, counsel and more, much, much more. The list of Gods gifts is innumerable, and He desires to give these to help establish His purposes in the earth. The Spiritual Gifts named in 1 Corinthians 12:7-10 can be placed into three different categories:

1. **Revelation-gifts**
    - Word of wisdom
    - Word of knowledge
    - Discerning of spirits

2. **Power-gifts**
    - Faith
    - Gifts of healings

- Working of miracles

3. **Speaking-gifts**
    - Speaking in tongues
    - Interpretation
    - Prophecy

God also gives seven other gifts for the empowerment of the Body of Christ. These are outlined in Romans and referred to a Motivational Gifts, because they motivate or spur us on to good works.

*"Having then **gifts differing according to the grace that is given to us**, whether **prophecy**, let us prophesy according to the proportion of faith; or **ministry**, let us wait on our ministering: or he that **teacheth**, on teaching; or he that **exhorteth** on exhortation: he that **giveth**, let him do it with simplicity; he that **ruleth**, with diligence; he that **showeth mercy**, with cheerfulness"* (Romans 12:4–8 KJV).

1) Prophesying - "If prophecy, in proportion to our faith."
2) Serving - "If service, in our serving."
3) Teaching - "The one who teaches, in his teaching."
4) Exhorting - "The one who exhorts, in his exhortation."
5) Giving - "The one who contributes, in generosity."
6) Leading - "The one who leads, with zeal."
7) Caring with mercy - "The one who does acts of mercy, with cheerfulness."

All the gifts of the Holy Spirit, whether manifestation gifts or motivational gifts, work together like the fingers of a hand: Each finger is important and has a different role and purpose, but only when these work together are God's purposes for the hand fully operational. The hand with all its fingers working together then builds great things on the earth. My fingers are working together to type this book. If I only used one finger, instead of ten, it would take a much longer time to complete. But with cooperation and synchronicity, the words flow onto the page.

When God created mankind, He certainly didn't plan for everyone to work on their own, detached from each other. Instead He planned teams and calls us together as team-players – humble people who depend on each other and both need each other to accomplish their purpose and assignments in the earth. Therefore, each person who intends to minister in the gifts of the spirit should operate in a spirit of humility, love, respect, honor and cooperation. We are better together and need one another. We should never compare and compete, but rather contrast and complete one another. This gives God the glory. God designed it this way, it helps govern us and requires us to be double dependent. This helps keep us humble. We are first, dependent upon God, second, interdependent upon others that He wants us to work with. This is how the five fingers on the hand lay hold of the hands purpose, all members working together as one. God writes the play from Heaven; He calls us as His actors on earth. If we are obedient to Heaven's script, we will "only do and say what the Father shows us" (John 5:19-20).

As team members we "speak the truth in love" and then "grow to become in every respect the mature body of him who is the head, that is, Christ. From him the whole body, joined and held together by every supporting ligament, grows and builds itself up in love, as each part does its work" (Ephesians 4:15-16 NIV). This is teamwork in action. Ask God to send your team members, and He will do it!

An Example of a spiritual gift I received by impartation

An example of a gift I received by impartation from the Lord is the writing gift. This was deposited in me as a seed. Just like an acorn grows into an oak tree, God's seed gifts on the inside of us can seem small at first, but then grow into great things. One day the Holy Spirit deposited in me the desire to write. As I prayed, I sensed him directing me to go to the typewriter. I had nothing to write, so I went back into prayer and I was shown an image of a thumbtack pointed toward heaven. I didn't know what this meant. As I prayed further the interpretation came to me. I got excited and ran to the typewriter and wrote my first teaching. It was a one-page message called "Thumbtack Faith." I penned what I saw; how some people's faith is like a thumbtack. They point their faith toward heaven, and they push it up, but it only goes about as far as a thumbtack. God's higher will is give us arrow faith; faith that soars in the heavenlies when it leaves our mouths in prayer and touches the throne room in Heaven that results in answers on earth.

I was so proud of my little teaching as a young Believer in Jesus. I approached another Christian who was more mature than me in the Lord and sought his counsel. He was in his 2nd year of Bible college. I proudly told him that God had given me a writing gift and that I was planning to write a book. I asked for his prayer of agreement to accomplish this task set before me. Instead of him praying with and for me, instead he looked down upon me with distain and said, "David, don't you think you should at least get a four-year seminary degree before you write a book? You don't have the authority to write a book for others to read until you've at least graduated from Bible College." The voice of worldly wisdom and religious requirements crushed my little ember of fire that was burning. In that moment my fire was put out. It took the wind out of my sails. His voice trumped the voice of God that had been speaking on the inside of me. I left without prayer and felt utterly dejected. This stalled me from writing anything else for nearly a year. His words and tone made me feel unworthy, inadequate and small, and I didn't want to lead anyone astray with my teachings because I hadn't been to a four-year Bible college. So, I attended Church and sat faithfully in Bible studies under other teachers. In addition, I also spent time studying God's word alone for several hours a day. During these study times and prayer, the Holy Spirit stirred inside me a second time. He was moving me to write again.

I immediately remembered the words of the seminary student and it stalled me from going to the typewriter a second time. I went back to prayer and as I began "praying in the Holy Spirit" something bigger than the voice of religion rose on the inside. A Holy Ghost boldness filled me, and I marched down to the typewriter and began to write. The words flew onto the page, it was like a fire shut up in my bones. A two-page teaching on faith was birthed! I shared this with others at a small Bible study. Their faith in Jesus soared and two were healed as we prayed together applying the Biblical principles from the teaching. God was moving!

My next teaching was a three-page document. Each one of these written teachings became a Bible study subject. Each week about ten to twelve men gathered and we studied the subject along with the Bible verses that supported the subject. Men began to grow in the Word, God began to set many free from sin issues, rejection, pride, anger, addictions and more. The Holy Spirit developed the writing gift inside me, and soon longer teachings, cleaner, clearer and more succinct came out through the typewriter. These teachings increased in size, and depth, and then became newsletters. A few years later a prison ministry was birthed using discipleship teachings and bonded-leather Study Bibles for those behind bars. Today this ministry, known as Heart of America Prison Ministries, reaches prisoners in more than 1,000 facilities with books, teachings and even Bibles. www.HeartPrisonMinistries.org Men and women's lives have been changed that began with a one-page teaching called, Thumbtack Faith. "Do not despise the day of small beginnings" (Zechariah 4:10).

Through the monthly donations of others, Heart of American Prison Ministries sends some of these prisoners the gift of a bonded-leather bound study. These hungry recipients who have requested to be placed on a Bible waiting list spend hours in these Bibles each day, just like I did. They are being changed into the image and likeness of Jesus in His presence. We've been able to send in more than 10,000 Study Bibles to individual prisoners through our not-for-profit organization, Heart of America Prison Ministries. I'm so glad the Holy Spirit stirred me to return to the typewriter a second time, or I'd still be sitting in Bible Study trying to be good enough for God to use me. What is God stirring inside of you? Don't allow another voice to stop you from stepping out of the boat and walking on the water with Jesus. He is able to keep you from falling, just keep your eyes on him while you walk. Do not allow another voice to hold you back from fulfilling your assignment in the earth. People who you've not yet met depend on the seed of God on the inside of you to become the oak tree of righteousness that will positively affect their lives.

As we "fan the flame" of the Holy Spirit on the inside of us it will grow and grow and grow. There are no limits with God. It begins with a seed planted on the inside of you. Protect it, pray over it, ask God to grow it in His presence.

The 5/25 Rule

A successful businessman was asked by his jet pilot the secret of his success. He said three words, "Focus, Focus, Focus." He continued, "You must apply the 5/25 Rule." The pilot said I don't understand. The businessman said, "I'm going to give you an exercise today. When I return to fly home, I want to examine your work. He continued, "Write down the 25 most important things you want to accomplish in your life before you die." He went on, "It could be owning your home debt free, getting another degree, starting your own jet charter company, sky-diving, planting an organic garden, or under-water-basket-weaving. It doesn't matter to me, it's whatever is most important to you." The pilot leaned back in his seat and then agreed to do the work.

The businessman returned to fly home and asked to review the pilot's homework. He handed the businessman his handwritten list of 25 things he wanted to accomplish during his life. The businessman examined these, smiled and said, "Well done. Now circle the top five things you want to accomplish first." The pilot paused, thought for a moment and then circled the top five of the twenty-five. The businessman then said, "Now, draw a line through each of the other twenty." The pilot said, "But I want to accomplish these also!" The businessman said, 'You will, after you accomplish these first five. In the meantime, each of the other twenty are distractions, these are your enemies that will cause you to lose focus on ever accomplishing the top five. Anything that keeps you from accomplishing your top five goals must be put aside. Focus, focus, focus. Once you accomplish one of the five, you can bring one of the twenty to the empty spot on your top five list and accomplish it also!" The pilot followed this principle and later owned his own charter company and several other things on the list.

Write, Write, Write

About three months ago, I sensed a stirring to write several small books on different subjects. I looked at my notes from the last 30 years, that began that day with Thumbtack Faith. The Holy Spirit highlighted a certain teaching in my files then began giving me additional revelation on the subject. I went to the computer and a book literally bubbled forth onto the pages. I published this on Kindle and in Paperback. While waiting for it to be approved, the Holy Spirit invited me to continue. There was more that He wanted to release through me from the Father's heart. I responded by leaning into prayer with Him and a few days later a second book was birthed. I put my hand to the plow. All my free time was spent in writing, writing, writing. Focus, focus, focus. I knew everything else was a distraction to what God was doing in and through my life in this season. This writing flow continued until ten books, on different subjects were birthed in forty-five days' time. Each of these books is now published on Amazon paperback and Kindle. People are now downloading and reading these books all over the world and sending emails through our ministry on how they've been impacted.

The anointing to write books lifted as quickly as it came. I began doing other things. The Holy Spirit sent me on another assignment through TV and Radio Broadcasts. Ninety days later I sensed the writing gift stirring inside me again. While sitting in the pew at a church service in prayer the Holy Spirit showed me a book. I saw the title and inwardly knew how to put the framework together. A few days ago, I went to the computer and began writing. This book is almost done and ready to go to press in only a few short days. To accomplish this so quickly, I decided to *focus, focus, focus.* This focus required me to avoid all unnecessary phone calls, text messages, dinner invitations, social media, TV, etc. But it was worth it, another book has been birthed that I believe will impact lives around the globe.

Partnering with the Holy Spirit

When we "hear God speak" and then "obey" (go and do what he shows us), Heaven's will is released into the earth through our actions. Partnering with God causes the work of our hands to become fruitful. We must learn how to flow in the times and seasons with God to know what and when to do certain things. This is called the anointing of the sons of Issachar. "And of the children of Issachar, *which were **men** that **had understanding of the times, to know what Israel ought to do**"* (1Chronicles 12:32 KJV). You can have this same anointing to know the times and seasons from the Holy Spirit by asking for it now. This is one way that God's gifts come to you and are deposited like a seed. Then, nurture the seed in prayer and see it grow for God's glory!

I share this example because God has given you gifts. When you spend time in prayer the Holy Spirit will speak to you. Once you hear Him speak, if you move into action, things will be birthed. It could be a business idea. An invention. A ministry. Ask God for wisdom and He will impart it to you just like He promises (James 1:5-8). Then you can "hear and obey" (John 2:5). Whatever Jesus tells you to do, just do it! Don't let the other voices deter you from conceiving in prayer and then birthing into the earth what God wants to release through you from Heaven. Go ahead, take a moment and ask now.

Prayer

God, I humbly but confidently ask You for the same anointing to know the times and seasons that You gave to the Sons of Issachar which gives the keen understanding of the timing and seasons of what and when I should put my hand, mind, time, talents and gifts to use with You. I ask You to stir inside me Your purposes that will move me to prayer and action. I ask You to release Heaven into the earth through my life, in Jesus Mighty Name. Amen.

Now watch what God does next in and through your life. He may speak to you in a dream tonight. I encourage you to put a pen and paper by your bed, or a voice recorder, or iPad, or something to help chronicle or record what he shows you. If you've never experienced or understood God speaking to you in dreams or visions of the night, I recommend my book on this subject. It outlines God's 7 Primary Purposes for Dreams and Visions. "Dreams and Visions" available on Kindle and paperback. (www.Amazon.com)

CHAPTER 12
PEOPLE MAY NOT ALWAYS UNDERSTAND OR AGREE WITH YOU

People may not always understand or agree with you, but don't let their voice deter you from what the Voice of God is speaking to you in the moment. The fruit of your decision to obey God will reveal His love and His wisdom for people in the earth. The man whose religious voice told me I needed a seminary degree before I could write a book was the voice of religion, and this well-meaning voice almost caused me to miss my assignment as a writer for Jesus in earth.

Jesus said that those who "hear and obey" the Spirit of God are not just children of God, but mature "**sons of God**". This maturity occurs when we are "led by the Spirit" (Romans 8:14).

God wants us to mature from lambs to sheep. Lambs aren't able to conceive and give birth because they aren't developed enough, but when lambs grow into sheep, they can give birth to baby lambs. This is maturity, bearing fruit after our own kind. Duplication and Multiplication. This is an example of "bearing fruit," and "fruit that remains." We grow in our faith over time. We begin with the milk of the Word, but then we learn how to chew and digest "strong meat" with maturity. "For every one that useth milk is unskillful in the word of righteousness: for he is a babe.[14] But strong meat belongeth to them that are of full age, even those **who by reason of use have their senses exercised to discern both good and evil**" **(Hebrews 5:13-14 KJV).** If we want to be able to distinguish God's voice from all the other voices of the world, we must spend time in God's word, both the milk, and the meat of His Word. Then we will learn to step out of the boat when we hear Jesus call us and walk on the water with him like Peter (Matthew 14:22-28). God will mature us from eaglets to Eagles and we will leave the nest where others are feeding us and then fly with Him and soar into our destiny!

Jesus spoke of those who were led by the Holy Spirit of God. He said, "The wind blows where it wishes, and you hear the sound of it, but cannot tell where it comes from and where it goes. **So is everyone who is born of the Spirit**" (John 3:8 NKJV).

The key to having a "living faith" is simple, we just keep our eyes focused on Jesus and what He is saying and doing in the moment. "As many as are led by the Spirit of God, these are the sons of God" (Romans 8:14 KJV). And don't take your eyes off Jesus or be distracted, delayed, stalled or derailed in your assignment by listening to the other voices contending for your attention. Otherwise you may sink into the very water Jesus has enabled you to walk with Him on by faith.

Focused obedience to what Jesus is saying and doing will sustain you and release the power of Heaven into the earth for others. This is why Jesus taught us to pray to the Father that "His will might be done in earth as it is in Heaven" (Matthew 6:11 KJV). The key to the miraculous is "hearing and doing" whatever Jesus tells us to do and say (John 5:19-20).

"Hearing and Doing"

An example of Hearing and Doing is demonstrated during Jesus first miracle of turning water into wine at a wedding celebration with his disciples.

"On the third day there was a wedding in Cana of Galilee, and the mother of Jesus was there. Now both Jesus and His disciples were invited to the wedding. And when they ran out of wine, the mother of

Jesus said to Him, "They have no wine." Jesus said to her, "Woman, what does your concern have to do with Me? My hour has not yet come." His mother said to the servants, **"Whatever He says to you, do it"** (John 2:1-5 NKJV).

This is the key to unleash the miraculous is twofold: (1) **Hearing** and **(2) Doing.** *Whatever Jesus says to you to do, do it!* It works every time, because it's His idea. You don't have to twist God's arm. He's looking for someone to agree with Him. This is how God's designed it to work, to release His will, purposes, plans, healings, provisions, miracles and more, "in earth as it already is in Heaven" (Matthew 6:11). Jesus spoke to the disciples and instructed them to fill the water pots with water. After they did this, Jesus didn't do the miracle. Instead there was **a second step of obedience**. They had to draw out the water and bring it to the governor of the feast. They had to do this by faith and not by sight. "And Jesus saith unto them, Draw out now, and bear unto the governor of the feast (v 8). They heard Jesus and acted; they **heard** and then **did** what he instructed, regardless if it made sense to their natural reasoning.

Result; the common water miraculously turned into the best tasting wine. "And they took *it.* When the master of the feast had tasted the water that was made wine…the master of the feast called the bridegroom. And he said to him, "Every man at the beginning sets out the good wine, and when the *guests* have well drunk, then the inferior. **You have kept the good wine until now!"** (v. 9-10 NKJV).

The Bible says, "This beginning of signs Jesus did in Cana of Galilee and manifested His glory; and His disciples believed in Him" (v. 11).

Hearing and **obeying** is a two-sided key that unlocks the door to the miraculous. This is by God's design. God gave us Jesus to role-model this for us. He did this for three and a half years of ministry, and then the disciples recorded it for us in the Bible. "Faith comes by hearing (reading)" (Romans 10:17). The good news is that God desires us to release His already decided will from heaven to earth through us. This is accomplished when we **hear** and **act**. Scripture says that Jesus was without sin (Hebrews 4:15).

"For we do not have a high priest who is unable to empathize with our weaknesses, but we have one who has been tempted in every way, just as we are—**yet he did not sin**" (Hebrews 4:15 NIV).

How was this possible? Jesus spent time in prayer daily with the Father, and was positioned to hear, and when He heard, He obeyed, regardless of the other voices that tried to influence Him. Jesus remained in perfect agreement with the Holy Spirit and the Father, even when He was required to bear His own cross on the road to Golgotha to be crucified for you and me. Jesus said these words about hearing and obeying the Father's will:

"Most assuredly, I say to you, the Son can do nothing of Himself, **but what He sees the Father do; for whatever He does, the Son also does in like manner.** For the Father loves the Son, and shows Him all things that He Himself does; and He will show Him greater works than these, that you may marvel" (John 5:19-20 KJV).

Jesus, our role-model, said before he went to the Cross in our behalf, "Most assuredly, I say to you, he who believes in Me, **the works that I do he will do also; and greater *works* than these he will do, because I go to My Father.** And whatever you ask in My name, that I will do, that the Father may be glorified in the Son." He continued, "If you ask anything in My name, I will do it *(John 14:12-14 NKJV).*

If you want to do the same kinds of miraculous works that Jesus performed and role-modeled, you can. This is God's desire for your life and for those around you. The keys to unleashing the miraculous are the same keys God has given you. "Only do what the Father shows you to do." This two-step process is demonstrated throughout the Bible. "Hearing and obeying" the voice of God releases the miraculous. This is how you deploy the authority within "the keys to the kingdom" that

Jesus gives to those who obey Him. " And I will give you the keys of the kingdom of heaven, and whatever you bind on earth will be bound in heaven, and whatever you loose on earth will be loosed in heaven" (Matthew 16:19 NKJV).

The Apostle Peter and John learned how to release the power of God afresh while entering the Temple Gate for prayer in Acts 3:1-11.

"Now Peter and John went up together to the temple at the hour of prayer, the ninth *hour*. And a certain man lame from his mother's womb was carried, whom they laid daily at the gate of the temple which is called Beautiful, to ask alms from those who entered the temple; who, seeing Peter and John about to go into the temple, asked for alms. And fixing his eyes on him, with John, Peter said, "Look at us." So he gave them his attention, expecting to receive something from them. **Then Peter said, "Silver and gold I do not have, but what I do have I give you: In the name of Jesus Christ of Nazareth, rise up and walk." And he took him by the right hand and lifted *him* up, and immediately his feet and ankle bones received strength.** So he, leaping up, stood and walked and entered the temple with them—walking, leaping, and praising God. And all the people saw him walking and praising God. Then they knew that it was he who sat begging alms at the Beautiful Gate of the temple; and they were filled with wonder and amazement at what had happened to him."

Peter and John were led by the Holy Spirit in what they **said** and **did**. True faith usually requires both, **speaking something** accompanied by **some type of action.** They **said, "In the Name of Jesus Christ of Nazareth, rise up and walk"** (v 6). After they spoke these words by the power of the Holy Spirit, then they took action. Faith is often an action. "**And he took him by the right hand and lifted him up,** and immediately his feet and ankle bones received strength" (v. 7).

This two-fold act (speaking and doing) released the miracle. Just like the water to wine miracle. It wasn't until they took the water to the head of the feast and told him to take some and drink it that the water turned to wine. Many miracles are short-circuited by failing to act. The book of Acts was written because the Apostles acted! They did the stuff the Holy Spirit spoke to them and God released miracles from Heaven! Hearing and Obeying, Hearing and Obeying, Hearing and Obeying. Therefore, we must learn to hear God's voice above all the other voices of the world.

The voice of religion tries to block miracles, but this religious voice can't stop the faith of others seeking God for their miracle, if they press through. Let's look at the crippled man who is lowered through the roof of a house by his four faith-filled friends to get him in front of Jesus for healing.

Jesus Forgives and Heals a Paralytic
Luke 5:17-26

"Now it happened on a certain day, as He was teaching, that there were Pharisees and teachers of the law sitting by, who had come out of every town of Galilee, Judea, and Jerusalem. **And the power of the Lord was *present* to heal them**. Then behold, men brought on a bed a man who was paralyzed, whom they sought to bring in and lay before Him. And when they could not find how they might bring him in, because of the crowd, they went up on the housetop and let him down with *his* bed through the tiling into the midst before Jesus. **When He saw their faith**, He said to him, "Man, your sins are forgiven you." And the scribes and the Pharisees began to reason, saying, "Who is this who speaks blasphemies? Who can forgive sins but God alone?" But when Jesus perceived their thoughts, He answered and said to them, "Why are you reasoning in your hearts? Which is easier, to say, 'Your sins are forgiven you,' or to say, 'Rise up and walk'? But that you may know that the Son of Man has power on earth to forgive sins"—He said to the man who was paralyzed, "I say to you, arise, take up your bed, and go to your house." Immediately he rose up before them, took up what he had been lying on, and departed to his own house, glorifying God. **And they were all amazed, and they glorified God and were filled with fear, saying, "We have seen strange things today!"**

The Bible says that **"The Power of God was present to heal them (the Pharisees and teachers of the law)"** (v. 17). But note; not one of the religious leaders received healing although, "the power of God was present *to heal them.*" Why? Because the religious voice in their ears hindered them from acting in faith to receive. Instead they were offended by Jesus. The crippled man's four friends, on the other hand, heard the voice of God in this moment, and acted. Their faith became aggressive. Because there was insufficient room due to the people filling the place, these four friends chose an alternate route. The went to the roof and removed roofing tiles to see and hear Jesus teach. Then they lowered their crippled friend down by ropes into the service in front of Jesus. Their extreme act of faith, in response to the leading of the Holy Spirit, resulted in an extreme miracle. In the companion passage of this story in the Book of Mark it says these words, **"When Jesus saw their faith**, he said to the paralyzed man, "Son, your sins are forgiven" (Mark 2:5 NIV). God did the miracle when he saw **their faith**! We learn from this passage that we can help release miracles for others with our faith when we 'hear and obey" whatever the Holy Spirit shows us to do and say. We can also deduce from this story that it is imperative we don't allow the other voices, especially the voice of religion, to hinder or block us from receiving from God.

In the Old Testament the Israelites missed their day of visitation repeatedly with God. The Psalmist records these words, "Yes, again and again they tempted God, **And limited the Holy One of Israel**" (Psalms 78:41 NKJV). They listened to the wrong voices and "limited the Holy One of Israel." As a result, they died in the wilderness instead of entering the land God promised them (Deuteronomy 6:22-24).

"And the LORD showed signs and wonders before our eyes, great and severe, against Egypt, Pharaoh, and all his household. Then He brought us out from there, that He might bring us in, to give us the land of which He swore to our fathers" (Deuteronomy 6:22-24).

Even though they saw signs and wonders, ate angel's food, drank water from the Rock and were delivered repeatedly when they cried out to God, they refused to enter into the promised land because of their unbelief. They listened to the wrong voice. Faith comes by hearing and hearing by the Word of God (Romans 10:17 KJV). Doubt and unbelief come by hearing and listening to the wrong voices. The New Testament highlights the unbelief of the children of Israel,

"For unto us was the gospel preached, as well as unto them: **but the word preached did not profit them, not being mixed with faith in them that heard it**" (Hebrews 4:2-3 KJV).

They missed their day of visitation because of their unbelief. They listened to the wrong voice. God still speaks today. The word he spoke to the Hebrews still resonates for our lives. He told them, "TODAY IF YOU HEAR HIS VOICE, DO NOT HARDEN YOUR HEARTS" (Hebrews 4:7 NIV).

The Bible commands us to "test every spirit" that speaks to us. The Bible is our standard and gives us God's template for life and godliness while on this planet. If we obey the Holy Spirit and His Word, we will have great victories. God has called you to greatness! (For more in insight on this subject of how to move through the voices and people blocking your miracle, I highly recommend by book, *"Are you Helping or Hindering,"* available on Kindle and paperback, www.Amazon.com).

Now that you know how to recognize and distinguish God's voice from all the other voices of the world it is time to take the mountain!

CHAPTER 13
CLIMBING THE SEVEN CULTURAL MOUNTAINS OF INFLUENCE

God wants us to ask Him for the mountain. Caleb was 80 years old when the Israelites entered the promised land. He had been 40 years in the wilderness with the others. He'd watched thousands of his family, friends and brethren die without entering into the promise. When they arrived, he immediately wanted to live on the mountain he saw named Hebron. He requested of Joshua," Now therefore give me this mountain" (Joshua 14:12 KJV). Joshua blessed him and then Caleb took it with the power of God at age 80!

"Hebron therefore became the inheritance of Caleb the son of Jephunneh the Kenezite unto this day, **because that he wholly followed the LORD God of Israel**" (v. 14 KJV).

Jesus' death on the Cross defeated the enemy and provided us with authority to retake promised land. We will have to drive out the inhabitants. But He wants us to take the land. He calls many of us to climb the seven mountains of influence in the earth. Once we take one or several of these mountains, He wants to release His voice through us to positively influence the people that stand on and below each mountain. God wants to set His children free, and He wants to put His words in our mouths to accomplish this. Hearing and Speaking. Hearing and Doing. He is looking for a few good men and women He can trust on these mountains. To accomplish this, we must "hear and obey" what He is showing and telling us to do, and then take the mountain! It may not be what seems normal, but it will have lasting fruitfulness if we obey.

The Seven Mountains of Cultural Influence

The Seven Mountains of Cultural Influence are: 1). Family, (2) Government, (3) Education, (4) Economy, (5) Church/Religion, (6) Arts and Entertainment, and (7) Media.

To effectively climb one or several of these mountains it will be necessary to recognize and distinguish the voice of God from all the other voices of the world. We will have to obey the voice of God above all others.

Each mountain will have a voice that offers you something to distract, hinder, offer, seduce or stop you from climbing higher. These voices may encourage you to pitch your tent or build a house at that place and dwell there. If you don't listen to the first voice that comes at you, another will try and distract you from your true purpose and assignment. If you continue to climb the enemy will see you as a threat and try to dissuade you himself. You may be offered the lust of the flesh (hedonism), the lust of the eye (materialism) or the pride of life (egoism). He may offer you "all the kingdoms of the world." No one is exempt from temptations on their climbs. But all have God's empowerment to overcome and receive the crown of life that Jesus promises you inside His Word to say, "It is written." And by the power of the Holy Spirit to say, "Get behind me Satan." If you have read this entire book, then I believe you are positioned to become one of God's overcomers! Which mountain is God calling you to take?

The Keys Of Authority Are In Your Hand Now.

The spiritual keys of authority to accomplish your assignment in the earth are in your hand, your voice, your mouth, your actions, your obedience to the Holy Spirit directing you to utilize these. Let's look at a few verses that reveal your authority from both Old and New Testaments:

Matthew 16:19: "I will give you the keys of the kingdom of heaven; whatever you bind on earth will be bound in heaven, and whatever you loose on earth will be loosed in heaven."

Isaiah 22:22 NIV: "I will place on his shoulder the key to the house of David; what he opens no one can shut, and what he shuts no one can open."

Revelation 3:7-8 NKJV: "These things says He who is holy, He who is true, "He who has **the key of David**, He who opens, and no one shuts, and shuts and no one opens": "I know your works. See, I have set before you an open door, and no one can shut it."

To best utilize these **spiritual keys of authority** we must overcome the voices of the enemy every step of the way. Distracting voices will hinder us from using our keys. Doors will remain locked to the supernatural which God promises for the situation. It is imperative we recognize and take every thought that comes to our mind and test it with God's Word. We must cast down every voice that is not in line with God's will, character, nature and role-model. Jesus said, "If you've seen me, you've seen the Father" (John 14:7-9). If we want to know the will of the Father, we have it recorded for us in Gospels with the life of His Son. This is the ultimate litmus test. Everything else speaking to us is another voice and must be ignored, silenced or destroyed in respect and obedience to the Father.

2 Corinthians 10:3-5 NIV: *"We are* destroying speculations and every lofty thing raised up against the knowledge of God, and *we are* taking every thought captive to the obedience of Christ, **and we are ready to punish all disobedience, whenever your obedience is complete."**

Listening to and acting on the Voice of God will silence and destroy all the other contending voices of the enemy. You are an overcomer. You have been given the keys to the kingdom. It's time to use these keys to open Heaven's doors with your authority and close and lock the doors of hell. Jesus said, "…On this rock I will build my church, and the gates of Hades will not overcome it" (Matthew 16:18 NIV).

Prayer for Keys

Heavenly Father, I ask You to give me the keys You have ordained for my life and assignment on the earth. Grant me wisdom and faith on how to best utilize these to open the doors of heaven and close the gates of hell. To hold back the plans of Satan and release the plans of Jesus. To set the captives free and empower the Believers to take the mountains and release the will of the Father. Grant me eyes to see and ears to hear what the Spirit is saying in this hour. I believe and receive the ability to hear and obey whatever is spoken to me from this day forward. I also now activate the voice of the shed blood of Jesus to speak in my behalf by coming into right standing with You. I bring all my issues into the light so the blood of Jesus can cleanse me from all the sin for which I was guilty. I appropriate the voice of Your Son's blood to adjudicate in my behalf over all the voices that have been speaking against me. The voice of the accuser of the brethren and the voice of religion that says, "I'm not good enough." Today I accept the blood of Jesus that trumps every other voice of the enemy and his cohorts, including the voice of hopelessness, fear, anxiety, torment, guilt, shame, condemnation, lust, mammon, pride, addiction, and every other voice that comes to mind as I pray this prayer. Thank you for declaring me innocent in Your sight. In Jesus Mighty Name and by the authority of this shed blood that speaks for me I declare myself free. And whom the Son makes free is free indeed! Amen and amen.

Jesus, I now fully trust You. I'm ready to use the keys take the mountain. Speak, for Your servant listens. I choose to hear Your voice and obey! Amen and Amen.

Giving and Receiving (Hearing and Obeying)

When we hear God speak, He will sometimes direct us to give, sometimes it's a small thing, other times it's a big thing. Hearing and obeying His voice in the small things will position us to move in authority over greater things. He usually starts us small, meeting us at our early levels of faith. Once we have exercised this faith level, our faith will increase. We will have history with God. Based on this history, trust (faith) increases again and again. He will usually ask us to do more each time. The good news is God never asks us to sow a seed unless he has a harvest on his mind. If we want to take the mountains it will require more faith. If we want to exercise authority over a place of influence, God will stretch us. This is often the way God works. Anything that is not of faith is sin (Romans 14:23). More will be required as we grow "from faith to faith" and "glory from glory." Jesus said these powerful words regarding the requirements to be trusted with increased authority from Him.

"For unto whomsoever **much** is **given**, of **him** shall be **much** required," (Luke 12:48 KJV).

A Practical Example

Every branch of our ministry, whether Bibles to Prisoners, Radio, Television, Books, Princess Crowning, online video platforms; each were birthed through prayer accompanied by sacrificial giving. When you are faithful with one thing, God will add another. The first ministry God conceived in me was the writing ministry. The second was the Bible ministry to prisoners. It was 1994 while I was serving a 22-year sentence in Federal Prison. The Holy Spirit instructed me to give my only Bible away to a prisoner. I immediately rejected this voice, confident it couldn't be the Lord. "I rebuke you Satan, the Bible says, "If I have two, I should give one to the man who has none." I only have one Bible and I will not give my only Bible away and be without God's Word." As I stood there pondering the still small voice that I'd heard, the Holy Spirit spoke a second time, "Give and more will be provided." A peace filled my soul. I then knew this was God and obeyed the Holy Spirit's instruction. I approached the prisoner the Spirit directed me to and handed him my Bible. I didn't know the man; he didn't know me. He looked at me perplexed. The Holy Spirit told me, "Tell him I forgive him, and I love him." When I told him these words he immediately burst into tears. I later learned that he was a backslidden Christian who'd fallen prey to another voice. He did a drug deal to provide for his lifestyle and ended up arrested in federal prison. When he received this Bible and heard these words of God's forgiveness, his life was instantly changed. My heart was filled with joy. I walked away.

He went to his room and began reading and reading and reading that Bible the rest of the night. At 4 AM the guards came and took him out of the prison. I don't know what happened to him, but he left with that Bible. The next day I called a friend named Kent by phone from prison. Kent said, "David, God spoke to me in a dream and instructed me to begin sending you $100 a month." He said, "You can use these funds monthly for whatever you want to buy at the commissary. I will send money every month until you are released from prison. I still had 14 years remaining on my sentence. Surprised by this, the Holy Spirit's words from the previous days were repeated, "Give and more will be provided." God's peace and joy flooded my soul again. I decided to use the $100 to purchase bonded leather-bound study Bibles for $25 each. I gave three away and kept the other for myself. The following month I used Kent's gift of $100 to buy four more Bibles. As the Holy Spirit directed, I gave each one away to prisoners. The next time I spoke to Kent by phone he told me the Holy Spirit asked him to increase his gift to $150 a month. I used the full $150 to buy more Bibles. Now six Bibles a month were going into the hands of the prisoners to help "equip the Saints for the work of ministry." Within a few months a genuine revival broke out at the prison. God began raising up disciples behind bars. Jesus was "changing lives, one Bible at a Time!" He was also answering the persistent prayers of mothers, fathers, and kids, and praying people everywhere in behalf of these lost sheep behind bars. This is the real story behind Heart of America Prison Ministries, how it was conceived by vision in 1990 and then birthed, in 1994, at a prison in Miami, Florida. To read the full story of the Holy Spirit revival at MCC Miami and the miracles that God performed across the federal prison system, I recommend my autobiography, *Jet Ride to Hell, Journey to Freedom* in paperback or on Kindle, www.Amazon.com). If you sense the Holy Spirit prompting you to help change lives behind bars through the gifts of a bonded-leather study Bible, you can give one time or monthly at www.HeartPrisonMinistries.org. You can also take a moment and ask the Holy Spirit if this a cause he wants you to partner with him on, *Helping "change lives, one Bible at a Time!"*

Another Example

While I was incarcerated, shortly after being born again in 1990, the Holy Spirit began to teach me about Biblical tithing. This was foreign to me, at first. I was in prison making only 12 cents an hour. I didn't have money to tithe. But I wanted to obey the Holy Spirit. Where He guides, He provides. I had to begin with what was in my hand. My first tithe was sent to a ministry using a book of stamps worth $5.80 at the time. Stamps were only .23 cents each then. I sent these stamps in an envelope to a ministry I had been ministered to through one of their teaching booklets I found at the Chapel library. The moment this envelope went into the prison mailbox, God spoke to a person to send me a money order. This arrived three days later. It was $58. Strange amount I thought. Then I remembered the $5.80, a tithe, one tenth of $58. The number matched 10X. Coincidence? Maybe, maybe not, but it sure set my faith on fire. As I prayed about what to do with the $58 the Holy Spirit showed me a need he wanted to meet on the prison compound. When men came into the prison, and several did each week, they had no hygiene items, and little to none were available for them from the prison. God wanted to solve this problem and meet their needs while demonstrating his love through provision. I had $58 in hand to partner with him. I went to the prison commissary and used $25 of the $58 to buy shower shoes, shampoo, deodorant, toothbrushes and toothpaste. The remaining funds purchased stamps for letters and additional items for my needs, including a few food items and hygiene stuff of my own. I then started a Christian locker in our unit of about 200 men. $25 didn't go very far, but God breathed on it. Other prisoners learned of this act and following this role model they began donating too. God began stirring their hearts, and they moved to action. Soon we had an abundance of hygiene products for the incoming prisoners. As the receivers were blessed by this act of kindness that came with no strings attached, they were touched, and they wanted to donate when they had funds. Soon there was a Christian locker in each of the four units on the compound.

Through this simple act of obedience, God opened the floodgates of giving. Men donated out of their available funds, men received what they needed from the Christian locker, and God began to financially bless men in prison. About two months later I received an unexpected money order for $250. This came from someone who had never sent me money before. They told me in a letter the Holy Spirit had been dealing with them to send me this $250 for about sixty days. The timeline matched. Coincidence? I don't know, but my faith soared again. I learned that God often speaks to people, stirs their hearts, but they don't always move into action. There is enough money in the earth to meet everyone's needs, but not everyone is listening to the Father's voice to release what is in their hands.

Shortly thereafter a revival broke out at this prison. Even the guards took note. Prisoners who didn't know each other cared for other prisoners through the Christian locker. Even non-believers were participating. It all started with a $5.80 book of stamps. I've learned that God usually only calls us to sow what he has already given us. If it's more than this, He'll put it in our hand. The widow gave her last meal of grain in her barrel to Elijah, and then God opened the floodgates of heaven and supernaturally provided for her with unlimited oil until the famine was over. She never went hungry again. Whatever is precious to you, and God asks you to give it up, when you do, you'll never run out of it again. God provided for me during my twenty years of incarceration, but he usually required me to step out on faith each time between harvests. And each time he called me to something new it resulted in an evangelistic impact or harvest of souls for His Kingdom. He's called you to do great things! Get ready!

Ceiled Houses

Last night before bed I was thanking God for the completion of this book. The only thing remaining was the conclusion and editing. This morning while was waking up, I heard the words "ceiled houses," and saw an additional chapter. I knew these two words were somewhere in the Old Testament but didn't know the exact context. As I opened my Bible app and did a search, I located these words in the Book of Haggai.

"Then came the word of the LORD by Haggai the prophet, saying, [4] Is it time for you, O ye, **to dwell in your ceiled houses,** and this house lie waste?" (Haggai 1:3 KJV).

As I continued to read, I discovered this passage speaks about giving and receiving. It deals with giving to the house of God. The passage continues with God asking the people to give for the purposes of His house. His house is a place where people can meet, fellowship, be taught the word of God, provisions can be given and handed out to those in need, and much, much more.

"Is it time for you yourselves to dwell in your paneled houses, and this temple *to lie* in ruins?" Now therefore, thus says the LORD of hosts: "Consider your ways!"

God was asking them to put Him first. God also told them to take a moment and "consider their ways." They were taking care of themselves first and forgetting about the needs on God's heart. He goes on to state that because they didn't put God first, the blessing of the Lord had lifted off their nation. God spoke clearly through the prophet Haggai to help redirect them to the blessing and deliver them from the consequences of listening to the other voices that had captured their attention.

"You have sown much, and bring in little;

You eat, but do not have enough;

You drink, but you are not filled with drink;

You clothe yourselves, but no one is warm;

And he who earns wages,

Earns wages *to put* into a bag with holes."

Thus says the LORD of hosts: "Consider your ways!"

(Haggai 1:5-7 NKJV).

Then God's voice reveals the problem and the solution:

"*You* looked for much, but indeed *it came to* little; and when you brought it home, I blew it away. Why?" says the LORD of hosts. "Because of My house that *is in* ruins, while every one of you runs to his own house. **Therefore the heavens above you withhold the dew, and the earth withholds its fruit. For I called for a drought** on the land and the mountains, on the grain and the new wine and the oil, on whatever the ground brings forth, on men and livestock, and on all the labor of *your* hands" (v. 8-1 NKJV).

Their actions of putting God second caused God to call for a drought over Israel. But now God wanted to lift the spiritual hindrance and release the blessing from heaven over their lives again. To accomplish this, **they would have to respond to His voice.** It would also require them to use the **keys of obedience in their hands;** they would have to release part of their substance to rebuild the house of God, to release the purposes and plans of God. A facility establishes stability, and enables the priests to release their abilities. A place where everyone could gather and worship, be taught the Word of God and learn how to pray, fast and obey directive of God. This place will also be a storehouse of food and goods to meet the needs of others who were less fortunate. A spirit of generosity would need to be released from the Spirit of the Lord to enable them to do this. God would have to "stir them up." As we see from Scripture this is exactly what God did.

"Then Zerubbabel the son of Shealtiel, and Joshua the son of Jehozadak, the high priest, with all the remnant of the people**, obeyed the voice of the LORD their God, and the words of Haggai the prophet**, as the LORD their God had sent him; and the people feared the presence of the LORD. Then Haggai, the LORD's messenger, spoke the LORD's message to the people, saying, "I *am* with you, says the LORD." So **the LORD stirred up the spirit of Zerubbabel** the son of Shealtiel, governor of Judah, and the spirit of Joshua the son of Jehozadak, the high priest, **and the spirit of all the remnant of the people**; and **they came and worked on the house of the LORD** of hosts, their God" (Haggai 1:12-15 NKJV).

The people obeyed the voice of the Lord coming through the words of Haggai the prophet. In response the Lord "stirred up the spirit of Zerubbabel and the people." The Spirit of the Lord often stirs us up once we agree to listen and obey his voice. When God speaks and we obey, the empowerment to establish God's will in the earth follows. This is a pattern we see throughout Scripture, from Genesis to Revelation.

Result: God rewarded the people for their act of obedience, sacrifice and love by sending his manifest and tangible presence; this is the Glory of the Lord. When God rests on the temple and people of this city, an open heaven is the result; the enemy is displaced, peace, prosperity, gold and silver is released to the people who obey and respond to His Spirit's stirring in their hearts.

"I will fill this temple with glory,' says the Lord of hosts. 'The silver is Mine, and the gold is Mine,' says the Lord of hosts. 'The glory of this latter temple shall be greater than the former,' says the Lord of hosts. 'And in this place I will give peace,' says the Lord of hosts" (Haggai 2:8-9 NKJV).

God does the same with us today, on different levels, and for different purposes. What is He speaking and stirring you to do? "God loves a cheerful giver!"

"But this *I say:* He who sows sparingly will also reap sparingly, and he who sows bountifully will also reap bountifully. *So let* each one *give* as he purposes in his heart, not grudgingly or of necessity; **for God loves a cheerful giver**. (2 Corinthians 9:6-7 NKJV).

The good news is when God stirs our hearts to give, he has a harvest on his mind.

And God *is* able to make all grace abound toward you, that you, always having all sufficiency in all *things,* may have an abundance for every good work" (v. 8).

If what's in your hand is too small to be your harvest, don't eat it, plant it! For those who have nothing to give, He will even place a seed in your hand, like he did with me; a $5.80 book of .23 cent stamps. When we sow the seed instead of eating the seed, God will make it multiply in ways that only He can do. And a harvest of souls will be added.

"Now may He who supplies seed to the sower, and bread for food, supply and multiply the seed you have *sown* and increase the fruits of your righteousness, while *you are* enriched in everything for all liberality, which causes thanksgiving through us to God" (2 Corinthians 9:6-11 NKJV).

Prayer for Seed and Planting

Heavenly Father, You said you love a cheerful giver. I want to be a cheerful giver. You also said You give seed to the sower. If you ask me to give more than I have I believe You'll put the rest my hand to fulfill the directive. Because this is in Your Word, I believe Your voice above all the other voices of the world. Based on Your Word I now ask You to place seed in my hand and give me a cheerful heart to give it where You are directing. Birth something in me, plant something through my hands and cause others to join in what You want to do in the earth. I ask this prayer right now by faith in Jesus Mighty Name. Amen.

CONCLUSION

The Bible reveals Seven Different kinds of voices. Each of these seven voices contend for our attention. If we recognize and obey the voice of God, we will have amazing results and experience a supernatural life. If we allow ourselves to be distracted or yield to the other voices of the world, problems will follow.

The Blood of Jesus also has a voice. His shed blood speaks on our behalf before the throne of Grace. His blood trumps (triumphs over) any other voice, including the voice of Satan, the accuser of the brethren. When we ask God for forgiveness for our wrongdoings from our heart and turn from these, the blood of Jesus is activated and speaks for us. We are then cleansed by this power from all unrighteousness. This repositions us to hear the voice of God accurately again. The Bible says,

"Behold, the Lord's hand is not shortened, That it cannot save; Nor His ear heavy, That it cannot hear. But your iniquities have separated you from your God; And your sins have hidden His face from you, So that He will not hear. For your hands are defiled with blood, And your fingers with iniquity; Your lips have spoken lies, Your tongue has muttered perversity" (Isaiah 59:1-3 NKJV).

Repentance Creates Divine Reset

Once we repent of all known sins, the blood of Jesus speaks for us to the Father and declares us "not guilty." God and you are back in perfect harmony. Repent means to "re" (return) to the "pent" (highest place, penthouse). When you repent, you agree with His voice above every other voice speaking to you; God restores you to the highest place with Him, in fellowship with God. The Holy Spirit then begins speaking

His desires and plans afresh for your life. His plans are always good for you (Jeremiah 29:10-13). He loves you just the way you are, but loves you way too much to leave you in your current condition. He loves communicating with you. He desires you hear His voice. The Holy Spirit enables you to hear Jesus speaking; either from the Bible while you read or directly by His still small voice. Praying in the Holy Spirit with your prayer language will help empower you on the inside and also move things in prayer and proclamation on the outside; preparing the way before you for victory. When we are led by the Spirit and in sync with Him, he will always "lead you in triumphal procession in Christ" (2 Corinthians 2:14).

Studying the Scriptures, prayer, fellowship, singing unto the Lord, fasting and praise, cheerful and sacrificial giving, will enable you to experience the tangible, life-changing power of God on a daily basis. "In His presence there is fullness of joy" (Psalms 16:11). In His presence there is also freedom, empowerment, peace, protection, power and so much more. In His presence you will hear His voice and be transformed into the image of Jesus, from "grace to grace," "faith to faith," "strength to strength," and "glory to glory." The path before you will grow brighter and brighter. From this relationship-based position of love and walk with Jesus, anything is possible!

You are ready to move into the higher realms with God. You are now educated and empowered to distinguish the Master's voice from all the other voices of the world. Every other voice becomes faint in the distance. The future is now bright!

God Bless,

David Hairabedian

Founder -VirtualChurchMedia.com and HeartPrisonMinistries.org

BONUS - SECTION 2
25 WAYS GOD SPEAKS TODAY

※

The below comes from my book, Hearing God 25 Different Biblical Ways. I've included this as a bonus section because I believe God wants to speak with you in a variety of ways. This will give you a Biblical basis for at least twenty-five ways He may communicate with you in the days ahead. You are a champion in the making!

25 WAYS GOD SPEAKS

1. Quickenings of the Holy Spirit

(Psalms 119:25, 50,107 KJV) – The first and most common way God communicates to us is through His written Word. I believe this accounts for the highest percentage of God's communication to His people. "This is my comfort in my affliction: *for thy word hath quickened me*" (v. 50). "Your word is a lamp to my feet and a light to my path" (v. 105). "…*Quicken thou me according to thy word*" (v. 25). The Holy Spirit is our Teacher. He "quickens" us through His Written Word. To quicken means to "*make alive, revive or bring to life.*" When we are faithful to read and study the Scriptures, the Holy Spirit is faithful to teach us. Whether lambs or sheep in our maturity level, the Holy Spirit meets us our own level and raises us to the next level, and the next and the next. While we grow in righteousness from faith to faith, none of us ever fully arrive in this life. The Christian walk is an ongoing growth process from glory to glory. We are always learning more.

Because of this, the same verse of Scripture we've read a dozen times before will suddenly come alive as the Holy Spirit illuminates, teaches, convicts, or directs us to some sort of action. It may be something as simple as fasting. When we obey this prompting, God's blessing will follow.

The Holy Spirit may have just convicted you while reading this last sentence. If so, this is likely God's voice calling you to a fast. Stop here and ask him how long He wants you to fast and for what reason. Then do whatever He says.

Always remember, the primary way in which God speaks to His childrenIs through the quickening of His written Word. All the other ways in which God speaks will come into alignment with His Written Word. Even when Jesus, our example, spoke to the disciples on the road to Emmaus shortly after His resurrection from the dead, He quickened the Written Word to their hearts. "And they said to one another, 'Did not our heart burn within us while He talked with us on the road, and while He opened the Scriptures to us'" (Luke 24:32, NKJV)? Once we are familiar with the written word — the standard for testing all other revelation — God will also begin speaking to us through a variety of other Scriptural ways to provide us with specific details for our lives and the lives of those around us. He might tell us a specific person to minister to and how to do it to bring them to Christ. Or, He might tell us who to marry, what house to buy, where or when to move, what stock to invest in, whom to do business with and who not to do business with, how much and where to give financially, what ministry, the timing and for what purpose. He may give us specific instruction on how to lay hands on a sick person to release Heaven's healing power, administer deliverance, or how to otherwise effectively pray for someone. When God speaks such specific things, we can search the Written Word for confirmation. "By this we know the spirit of truth and the spirit of error" (1John 4:6). With this foundation properly established, we now move on to the various other ways God speaks today.

2. Internal Unctions

The second most common way God speaks to us is through ***the unction of the Holy Spirit***. "But ye have an ***unction*** from the Holy One, and ye know all things" (1John 2:20, KJV). The Holy Ghost ***unction*** enables us to know things supernaturally that cannot otherwise be known or naturally explained. As we mature the unction of the Holy Spirit will begin to provide more detailed information through the revelation gifts of the Spirit; word of knowledge, word of wisdom, discerning of spirits, and prophecy (see 1Corinthians 12:7-10).

While we are still baby lambs the Holy Ghost unction will usually come with less details than this, and often in more subtle ways. For example, we might find ourselves saying, "I don't know how I know, but I just know!" This is usually the Holy Spirit's unction giving our hearts a witness that something is true. On the other hand, the Holy Spirit might also give us a check or a caution in our spirit that something is not true or is in error. One preacher describes this internal unction as the green light that tells us to go, the red light that tells us to stop and the yellow light that says to proceed with caution. Some people refer to this as being their intuition. Still others refer to this as the inward witness of the Holy Spirit. The King James Version of the Bible calls it the **unction of the Holy Spirit**. The New International Version calls it an anointing from the Holy One. "But you have an anointing from the Holy One and you know all things" (1John 2:20, NIV). Some Christians say, "I just know in my knower." Regardless of the terminology we use to identify this avenue of God speaking to us, Biblically we can agree that the source of this inward knowing is the Third Person of the Trinity. This is the Holy Spirit communicating Heaven's will to our human spirit so we can effectively live the Christian life. When we obey God's voice speaking to us through this inward way, things usually work out very well. When we ignore (or disobey) this unction, things many times turn out very badly. Most prisoners I've spoken with have said, "I knew something was wrong just before I got arrested, but I ignored my gut feeling about it and here I am."

God even speaks to sinners through such conviction, at times, to warn them of impending doom. I know He clearly spoke to me this way while I was deep in sin, but I shrugged it off and disobeyed. Here I am too! The old adage applies here, "Fool me once, devil, shame on you. Fool me twice, shame on me." May we all learn to recognize and heed God's voice speaking to us today and every day in the future until Jesus' return.

3. Perceiving

This is like an unction, but it usually comes with more details. Before Paul boarded the ship as a prisoner on his way to Rome, he advised the Captain, saying, "Men, *I perceive* that this voyage will end with disaster and much loss, not only of the cargo and ship, but also our lives." (Acts 27:10, KJV). Paul received a word of knowledge that provided him with specific details concerning disaster and loss if they proceeded further on the voyage. The Holy Spirit provided Paul with an **inward perceiving** that things were about to go awry. The centurion of the ship ignored Paul's words of warning.

"The centurion was more persuaded by the helmsman and the owner of the ship than by the things spoken by Paul" (v. 11).

Therefore the Bible says, "Trust in the Lord with all your heart, and lean not on your own understanding; in all your ways acknowledge Him, and He shall direct your paths" (Proverbs 3:5-6).

Because the centurion disobeyed the inward perceiving Paul received from the Lord, the ship and its 276 passengers later sailed into disaster. When this occurred, because Paul had previously announced the problem, Paul was able to speak a second time with more authority, "Men, you should have listened to me, and not have sailed from Crete and incurred this disaster and loss" (v. 21). Paul not only spoke a second time, but also began to fast and intercede during the storm, praying for everyone's deliverance. Fourteen days later, God responded to Paul's prayer by speaking again. This time God sent Paul a visitation from a messenger angel (see also no. 13 below) with additional instructions from heaven. "Do not be afraid, Paul; you must be brought before Caesar; and indeed, God has granted you all those who sail with you" (v. 24). Paul communicated God's message to the centurion in charge. The centurion took heed this time, obeying the voice of God speaking through Paul, and everyone on board was saved! The entire ship and its contents, however, were lost in the sea (v. 44).

When we obey such "inward perceivings" given to us by the Spirit this will help us to avoid unnecessary shipwrecks and related losses.

4. God's Still Small Voice

This is another common way that God speaks to His children. When the Holy Spirit's still small voice speaks to us, it usually comes with specific words in our spirit. It may be a single word, a sentence, a phrase, or a full paragraph of communication. The Holy Spirit speaks these words to our human spirit, and they rise or float upwards into our mind and understanding. We hear His voice in our spirit, where the Holy Spirit resides on the inside of us. Then, as these words float or rise up into our minds, they provide us with a message, instruction, direction, or an understanding on a matter. This is not to be confused with our regular thoughts or words we sometimes hear in our mind. This is usually the voice of our own soul, our fleshly thinking, the world, or our enemy, the devil. God's still small voice comes ***from inside our spirit*** and rises into our thinking, whereas the devil's voice speaks to us ***from outside our person*** and into our head. Elijah experienced the still small voice of God.

"And behold, the Lord passed by…but the Lord was not in the wind; and after the wind an earthquake, but the Lord was not in the earthquake…but the Lord was not in the fire; and after the fire ***a still*** *small voice*. So it was, when Elijah heard it, that he wrapped his face in his mantle and went out and stood in the entrance of the cave. And suddenly a voice came to him..." (1Kings 19: 11-13, KJV).

God was not in the wind, earthquake, or fire, but manifested Himself in a still small voice to Elijah. God's ***still small voice*** will line up with His written Word and is accompanied by supernatural peace. One way to discern the Lord's voice from the other voices of the world is this. The Holy Spirit convicts, leads, guides, directs, prompts, and occasionally prods us. The devil's voice, on the other hand, pushes, condemns, and brings anxiety to our souls. The devil's voice also results in fleshly works, pride, and the glorification of man instead of God. The devil's goal is to get us to place confidence in ourselves instead of God. Why?

Because the devil knows that if he can tempt us to miss the mark (sin) in this way, it will result in Heaven's judgment against us. An example of this is found in the Old Testament. King David was tempted by Satan to number his army. This was a fleshly work and resulted in judgment. "Now Satan stood up against Israel and moved David to number Israel" (1Chronicles 21:1, NKJV).

"And God was displeased with this thing; therefore, He struck Israel" (1Chronicles 21:7, NKJV). We must learn to distinguish between the Lord's voice and the enemy's voice. Obeying God's voice brings blessing while obeying the devil's voice brings a curse. "God resists the proud but gives grace to the humble. Therefore, submit to God. Resist the devil and he will flee from you" (James 4:6-7, NKJV).

5. Bearing Witness with Our Spirit

"The Spirit Himself ***bears witness*** with our spirit that we are children of God" (Rom. 8: 16, NKJV). The Holy Spirit bears witness when something is of God. He is the Spirit of Truth. This goes along with the above ***internal unction*** and ***inward perceiving***, and every

Born-Again Believer has this ***inward witness*** to truth in their born-again spirits. An example of this might be: when someone is speaking truth, whether from the pulpit or in an everyday conversation, the Holy Spirit will **bear witness** with our human spirit that this is truth. At times, our spirit's may even "amen" what is spoken before we understand with our minds what has been said. Just the opposite will also occur when error is spoken. The Holy Spirit gives us a check or a caution in our spirit that something isn't quite right. This also may occur before the person finishes speaking, or maybe even before they begin to talk! This is God protecting us. When we obey, we are blessed; when we disobey, things don't go so well.

6. Songs in the Night

" Where is God my Maker, Who gives ***songs in the night***" (Job 35:10, NKJV).

God will sometimes speak to us as we sleep by singing in our spirits ***a song in the night***. It could be a song of deliverance, peace, wisdom, forgiveness, victory, encouragement, or faith. Sometimes He even serenades us as His Bride, the Bride of Christ. When we wake up from an evening of songs in the night, we find ourselves rested and refreshed, ready for the day. This causes us to have God's words in our mouths for the day.

7. In Our Ear as We Wake in the Morning

"He awakens me morning by morning, he awakens my ear to hear as the learned" (Isaiah 50:4, NKJV). Many times, when we are waking up in the morning, somewhere between that sleep-state and being awake, God will speak in our ear with an instruction, warning, or word of encouragement for the day. This causes us to have God's words in our mouths for the day.

8. In Our Ear as We Sleep in the Night

"...when deep sleep falls upon men, while slumbering on their beds, then *He opens the ears of men* and *seals their instruction* (Job 33:16 NKJV). God often speaks to us at night when all the other voices of the world have fallen silent and our mind is calm. For many of us this is about the only time God can get through to us because we're so busy with the cares of the world throughout the waking hours of our regular day. When God speaks to us in this way upon arising from sleep, we should immediately get up and write down the sealed instruction given to us from the Spirit. If we are lazy and fall back asleep, we will usually forget part, or all, of the message, or think the instruction wasn't from the Lord in the first place. This will cause us to miss God's best in the situation. I recommend a pencil and paper be kept next to your bed each night before going to sleep. We never know when God may choose to speak to us. We should always be prepared to hear from God. And then, when He does speak, "Whatever Jesus says for you to do, do it" (John 2:5). the things which I have made touching the king: my tongue is the pen of a ready writer" (Psalms 45:1, KJV). When we've been in touch with the King our tongue is ready to speak the words of God. "Whoever speaks must do so as one speaking the very words of God" (1Peter 4:11, NRSV).

9. Visions

"I saw a dream which made me afraid, and the thoughts on my bed and the *visions of my head* troubled me" (Daniel 4:5). God will sometimes speak in visions. Visions can occur while sleeping (Daniel 4:5), praying (Acts 10:10), or at any time (John 5:19). Visions come in four main ways: (1) *open visions* (such as an appearance of an angel): (2) *trance visions* (such as Peter experienced on the roof of a house during prayer when God showed him four-footed unclean animals coming down from heaven on a sheet telling him to "kill and eat," meaning Peter was to take the Gospel to the Gentiles) (Acts 10:10); (3)

spiritual visions (such as occur while praying and the recipient is awake when God reveals His will in a matter) (John 5:19); and (4) ***visions of the night*** (such as King Nebuchadnezzar received during Daniel's days) (Daniel 4:5).

When receiving God's communication through visions, dreams, or other prophetic gifting, it's important to follow the ***three components principle of interpretation*** before acting on the message. The three components of interpretation are: (1) **Revelation**, (2) **Interpretation**, and (3) **Application**.

Revelation: We must first determine if the revelation is from God, the devil, our flesh, soulish thinking, or too much pizza and ice cream before bed. Once we have confidence it's a message from God, we can proceed to the second component.

Interpretation (what does this word, biblical symbol, or message from God mean?): If we don't have an accurate interpretation, we may have to pray for more understanding from the Lord. If we receive a clear interpretation or understanding, then and only then can we proceed to the final component of application. **Application** (what do we do with this information?): Proper application includes asking, "Does God want me to share the message with a specific individual, a group of people, a congregation, a leader, or a possibly a nation?" Or, could God be asking us to remain silent publicly and instead intercede privately in another's behalf? Or, is He asking us to go and do what has been spoken? Possibly, an act of kindness, a deed of mercy, meeting a financial need, or it may be casting out a demon to set someone free through the authority given to us in Jesus' Name. He may also ask us to give someone a warning to help avert disaster or he may be sending us to anoint someone who is sick with oil, praying the prayer of faith over them for healing, or some other supernatural release of God's power to His people. They key to experiencing the miraculous is simply this, "whatever Jesus tells you to do, do it!" (John 2:5)

10. Dreams

(Acts 2:17; Matthew 1:20; 2:13, 20, 22)

"For God may speak in one way, or in another, yet man does not perceive it.

In a dream, in a vision of the night, when deep sleep falls upon men, while slumbering on their beds, Then He opens the ears of men, and seals their instruction" (Job 33:14-16). Nearly one third of the Bible is compiled from dreams and visions given to men, women, prophets, prophetesses, godly and ungodly kings and queens, soldiers, etc. God still speaks this way today, if we'll only pay attention. One key to receiving a message from God through dreams is to put a pencil and paper next to your bed before going to sleep at night. This is an act of faith. When God sees us preparing to receive from Him, He often begins communicating through Heaven's language of the night. Then when God speaks, we put faith into action by writing the dream down as Scripture commands us (Daniel 7:1, Habakkuk 2:2-3).

Then we can follow the *three **components principle*** (see no. 9 above) to properly interpret and apply what God is speaking to us through pictures, scenes, and symbols. Did you know that you spend nearly one third of your life asleep? The average person sleeps approximately 8 hours of every 24-hour day. Over a period of 60 years, this means that you will be asleep for about 20 years. God wants to speak to communicate to us while we sleep.

Have you been listening?

11. Glimpses in the Spirit

(John 5:19) "Now we know only a little, and even the gift of prophecy reveals little! "Now we see things imperfectly as in a poor mirror, but then we will see everything with perfect clarity. All that I know now is partial and incomplete, but then I will know everything completely, just as God knows me now" (1Corinthians 13:9,12). Sometimes God graces us with a glimpse of something in the Spirit. This can be a brief image, picture, frame, or snapshot of information that reveals Heaven's will on a matter or warns us of the enemy's plan. When this occurs, we need to follow the ***three components principle*** to properly interpreting and applying what the Holy Spirit is revealing in that moment and then release Heaven's will into the earth by obeying God's instruction. God will also often grace us with a glimpse in the Spirit to bring us into closer fellowship with Him.

Once we receive the glimpse, then we are compelled into His presence for further revelation, interpretation, and application. At times, God will also give us a glimpse in the spirit that reveals the enemy's plans. He does this to protect us and fulfill His promise that he will not allow us to be "ignorant of the enemy's devices" (2Corinthians 2:11). Such glimpses help us thwart the enemy's plans and simultaneously release Heaven's plans into the earth in their place. Through this avenue of God speaking to us, the result is often God's will being accomplished in earth as it is in Heaven, just as Jesus taught us to pray in the Lord's prayer (Matthew 6:11). In such situations, it is important that we cooperate with God to release His will. Otherwise, we can short circuit God's plans through our in-action, miss-action, or anti-action. We can either agree with God's plan on the matter or the enemies. We can either walk with God or the adversary of our souls. "Can two walk together except they are agreed" (Amos 3:3)? Agreeing with God is the key to displacing the enemy's plans and releasing God's plans into the earth in Jesus' Name.

12. Trances

Peter experienced a trance vision while he was on the rooftop waiting for dinner (Acts 10:10-16 NKJV):

"Then Peter became very hungry and wanted to eat; but while they made ready, he fell into a trance and saw heaven opened and an object

like a great sheet bound at the four corners, descending to him and let down to the earth. In it were all kinds of four-footed animals of the earth, wild beasts, creeping things, and birds of the air. And a voice came to him, "Rise, Peter; kill and eat." But Peter said, "Not so, Lord! For I have never eaten anything common or unclean." And a voice spoke to him again the second time, "What God has cleansed you must not call common." This was done three times. And the object was taken up into heaven again.

The interpretation of this trance vision was that God was accepting the Gentiles for salvation. Its proper application was for Peter a Jew who didn't associate with non-Jews (Gentiles)] to begin preaching the Gospel of salvation to non-Jews. "While Peter thought about the vision, the Spirit said to him, 'Behold, three men are seeking you. Arise therefore, go down and go with them, doubting nothing; for I have sent them'" (Acts 10:19-20, NKJV).

Peter went to the house of Cornelius and God did a mighty work among the Gentiles. "While Peter was still speaking these words, the Holy Spirit fell upon all those who heard the word. And those of the circumcision who believed were astonished, as many as came with Peter, because the gift of the Holy Spirit had been poured out on the Gentiles also" (Acts 10:44-45).

Thank God Peter didn't dismiss this message from God as just being a fleshly reaction to his hungry stomach. Instead, he followed the three principles to properly interpret a vision (see part one for details): **1) revelation, 2) interpretation and 3) application**, and the Gospel was poured out on the Gentiles! We never fully know what may occur when we properly receive, interpret and apply a vision from God.

While trance visions can come at any time, including waiting for dinner, they usually occur

These experiences are so real that you usually not only see and hear, but also feel and smell everything in the scene, sometimes leaving your body reverberating from the Spirit's visitation. Trance visions are one of the most intense experiences a person can receive from God, often leaving a person shaken for several hours or even days (see Daniel 10:1-8; Ezekiel 3:10-15).

13. Through Messenger Angels

(Acts 27:23-25; Luke 1:12-20; 1:26-38)

As discussed in Paul's experience on the ship (see #3 above), Paul first "perceived" things were about to go wrong. Then after the storm began, Paul prayed and fasted. In response to Paul's prayers, God spoke by sending a messenger angel. "For there stood by me this night an angel of the God to whom I belong and whom I serve, "saying, `Do not be afraid, Paul; you must be brought before Caesar; and indeed, God has granted you all those who sail with you'" (Acts 17:23-24, NKJV).

Because "faith comes by hearing God speak," this angelic visitation empowered Paul to be able to confidently say, "Therefore, take heart, men, for I believe God that it will be just as it was told me" (Acts 27:25, NKJV). When the Centurion obeyed Heaven's words spoken through Paul, the plans of the enemy were thwarted, and God's plans prevailed. All 276 passengers were saved! In response to prayer and while in prayer. In such situations, God's Spirit causes us to fall into a brief trance and something like a movie scene opens up in our minds.

Paul communicated God's word to the Centurion. The Centurion obeyed the Word of the Lord through Paul, and then God's will was then "done in earth as it was in heaven." All the passengers were saved.

God still sends messenger angels today, because Jesus is "the same yesterday, today and forever" (Hebrews 13:8). Messenger angels, however, are usually for special situations, such as announcing the coming of Jesus, prophetic warnings for the future, or situations involving life and death. So, when you do receive a messenger angel, you can be rest assured that it's not just for your entertainment. We are either in the midst of some rough sailing like Paul, or God is preparing us for some rough seas ahead. His Voice is speaking to build our faith to prepare us for the incoming storm.

14. Visitations of the Lord

Paul received a personal visitation from Jesus on the road to Damascus (Acts 9:3-7). This experience forever changed his life. He went from a persecutor of Jesus and His Church to a mighty defender of and martyr for the Christian faith. A visitation from Jesus will always leave you strengthened in your faith and forever changed. The disciple Thomas was changed from a doubter to a faithful believer when Jesus appeared to him in bodily form after the resurrection (John 20:26-28). After this visitation from Jesus, Thomas was so strengthened in his faith that he preached the Gospel all the way to India, where he was eventually martyred at Madras for preaching Jesus as the One True God amidst a pagan nation that worshiped 3 million false gods. Foxes Book of Martyrs records another example of a post-resurrection visitation from Jesus to the Apostle Peter:

"In this persecution, among many other saints, the blessed apostle Peter was condemned to death...Hegesippus saith that Nero sought matter against Peter to put him to death; which, when the people perceived, they entreated Peter with much ado that he would fly the city. Peter, through their importunity at length persuaded, prepared himself to avoid. But, coming to the gate, he saw the Lord Christ come to meet him, to Whom he, worshipping, said, 'Lord, whither dost thou go?' To whom He answered and said, 'I am come again to be crucified,' By this, Peter, perceiving his suffering to be understood, returned into the city. Jerome saith that he was crucified, his head being down and his feet upward, himself so requiring, because he was (he said) unworthy to be crucified after the same form and manner as the Lord was." (Foxes Book of Martyrs, The Early Christians, the Execution of Peter, pp. 12-13).

To willingly turn ourselves in to the authorities when we know we will be sentenced to the death penalty would take a visitation from Jesus! Hearing Jesus speak brought faith for Peter's obedience unto death. Since Jesus is "no respecter of persons" He also promised us that if we would keep His commandments, He would manifest (reveal) Himself unto us. "He who has my commandments and keeps them, it is he who loves Me. And he who loves Me will be loved by My Father, **and I will love him and manifest Myself to him**" (John 14:21 NKJV). This promise is for every blood-washed believer, including you and me!

15. Through Signs and Wonders

On the day of Pentecost, Peter said that God spoke to us through signs and wonders that Jesus performed. "Men of Israel, hear these words: Jesus of Nazareth, a Man attested by God to you by **miracles, wonders, and signs which God did through Him in your midst**, as you yourselves also know" (Acts 2:22, NKJV).

In the first century, God continued to speak to the thousands of people through various signs and wonders done through the hands of the apostles, prophets, and evangelists and even lay ministers such as Stephen. "And Stephen, full of faith and power, did great wonders and signs among the people" (Acts 6:8, NKJV). Because of these wonders and signs, many people believed in Jesus as Lord and Savior. Sadly, however, not everyone recognizes God's voice through demonstrations of the Spirit's power, signs, and wonders. Instead, they persecute God's miracle workers and reject the message. "Then they cried out with a loud voice, stopped their ears, and ran at him with one accord; and they cast him out of the city and

stoned him" (Acts 7:57-58, NKJV). Because Jesus is "the same yesterday, today and forever" (Hebrews 13:8), He continues to speak through signs and wonders today. Some people respond and give their lives to Christ, while others reject the word of the Lord and persecute His messengers.

Always remember, a sign points to something greater than itself. For example, if a McDonald's sign says, "Free Big Mac's, 3 miles ahead," it would be foolish to simply sit around the foot of the sign, believing you will be fed there. A wise person **would obey what the sign is saying**. The sign is pointing to something greater than the wood, the picture and the paint. In this case, the sign is pointing three miles ahead. All who can read and obey the sign will travel the three miles, get a free Big Mac, and be full! So, it is today with signs, we must go to where the sign points: Jesus! If you get signs in your life, don't get stuck at the sign, but obey what the sign says, and get fed by the one to whom the sign points, Jesus!

16. Through our Five Spiritual Senses

This is one avenue of God's voice that some people experience more than others. Spiritual smell, touch, taste, hearing, and sight take some time to properly recognize. The author of Hebrews tells us how we grow in this discernment, "For everyone who partakes only of milk is unskilled in the word of righteousness, for he is a babe. But solid food belongs to those who are of full age, that is, those **who by reason of use have their senses exercised to discern both good and evil**" (Hebrews 5:13, NKJV). By using or exercising our spiritual senses, God will mature us in discerning both good and evil. At times, God will enable us to visually see a spiritual mantle of authority, anointing, or presence of the Holy Spirit on a preacher, teacher, or prophet (2Kings 2:15). One example of seeing into the spirit realm is found in 2 Kings: "And Elisha prayed, and said, 'Lord, I pray, open his eyes that he may see.' Then the Lord opened the eyes of the young man, and he saw.

And behold, the mountain was full of horses and chariots of fire all around Elisha" (2Kings 6:17, NKJV). The angels were there all the time. God gifted Elisha to see them. Their presence gave Elisha peace and confidence that God was with him. The young man couldn't see them until Elisha prayed for this gift to be given to him too. When this occurred, this young man's faith level skyrocketed. Angels and demons are always around us, we just can't see them with our natural eyes. If we simply ask God, He may open the eyes of our spirit to see them. If this occurs, it will encourage you in your faith and/or empower you to deal with the evil. Spiritual sight is one of the gifts of the Holy Spirit Paul refers to as discerning of spirits (1Corinthians 12:10).

Such spirits can be discerned, or distinguished by spiritual sight, touch, hearing, and even smell. For example, sometimes the Lord will open our spiritual senses to smell the unique fragrance of the Holy Spirit to confirm His presence. He will also open our spiritual senses to identify unclean spirits, and they usually have a very foul odor. (This is why some religions include incense in their services, to cover up the smell of demons who respond to their worship). Distinguishing of spirits will enable you to be prepared for what is about to occur next. Your spirit-man has all five senses in the realm of the spirit just as your natural-man has these same five senses in the natural realm. Don't limit God, but remember, we are required to test the spirits in every matter (see 1John 4:1-6). This is part of our growth and maturity (from baby lambs to young-adult sheep) in the Lord.

17. We Hear Incompletely

Sometimes we only hear **a portion** of what is needed. "For we know in part and we prophesy in part" (1Corinthians 13:9 KJV). I believe God sometimes reveals things to us in part, to draw us closer to Him in relationship through more fellowship and prayer. Proverbs says, "It is the glory of God to conceal a matter, but the glory of kings is to search out a matter" (Proverbs 25:2, NKJV).

When we seek God for more information, revelation, or understanding regarding a matter He spoke to us in part, He will often help us to find it. It may come through studying more of the Scriptures on the matter, and the Holy Spirit's quickening of something from the Bible, or it may come by more revelation from the Lord through the various other ways in which God speaks. On the other hand, it may not come until days or months later.

Jeremiah waited ten days for God to respond to him (Jeremiah 42:7). God wants us to persevere when seeking revelation from Him. Daniel waited 21 days time (Daniel 10:12-13). In this situation, the devil's evil angel withstood God's answer. The key here is to be patient and trust God. Don't lose hope if you don't receive an immediate response from God. "But those who wait on the Lord shall renew their strength" (Isaiah 40:31, NKJV). Remember, it is through faith and patience, we inherit the promises of God (Hebrews 6:12).

18. Through Dark Speech

God speaks to most of us in what the Bible refers to as "dark speech," meaning the message is not always 100 percent clear. "I will incline my ear to a proverb; **I will disclose my dark saying on the harp**" (Psalms 49:4, NKJV).

The term **dark saying,** or **dark speech** indicates a need for further illumination to fully understand the message. I believe God sometimes speaks this way to draw us closer to Him in fellowship before He releases more understanding. "It is the glory of God to conceal a matter, but the glory of kings is to search out a matter" (Proverbs 25:2, NKJV). God doesn't hide things from us, but for us, so we can discover them as we search them out.

God begins the process by speaking. We respond by seeking His Face. God then gives us more understanding on the matter. As stated above there are usually three components to fully understanding a prophetic word: **(1) revelation, (2) interpretation, and (3) application**. During Moses' day, God spoke with many of the prophets through dark sayings that came in the form of dreams or visions, which needed interpretation. Moses, on the other hand was God's special prophet and friend. God spoke to him face-to-face. "Hear now My words: If there is a prophet among you, I, the Lord, make Myself known to him in a vision, and I speak to him in a dream. Not so with My servant Moses; he is faithful in My entire house. I speak with him **face-to-face**, even plainly, and not in **dark sayings**; and he sees the form of the Lord. (Numbers 12:8, NKJV). Moses heard God's voice plainly. God spoke to Moses face-to-face (audibly) as a man speaks to his friend. There was no interpretation necessary with this level of revelation, whereas with dark sayings, visions, dreams, glimpses in the spirit and trances as mentioned in #'s 9, 10, 11 & 12 above) we usually have to seek God's face for further understanding and proper application of the revelation given to us. Again, I believe God does this to draw us into fellowship with Him because He loves spending time with us one-on-one, speaking to us and teaching us the things of His Kingdom.

19. We Don't Hear, But the Spirit Intercedes for Us

This can involve inward groanings in prayer, intercessory prayer or even praying in other tongues (which is one of the other gifts of the Spirit Paul mentions in 1Corinthians 12:7-10). "Likewise, the Spirit also helps in our weaknesses. For we do not know what we should pray for as we ought, but **the Spirit Himself makes intercession for us** with groanings which cannot be uttered. (Romans 8:26, NKJV). Again, this is a faith-builder. Remember, "faith comes from hearing" (Romans 10:17). Having the knowledge that the Spirit is interceding for us (and through us) in this unique manner also provides confirmation and peace that God has things under control. Sometimes He keeps certain information **from us** because it is too much **for us** to handle at the time. In such situations, if He did reveal the entirety of the matter, we would become more of a hindrance than a benefit in prayer. Our natural reasoning would impede the work of the Holy Spirit's flow in and through us.

20. Through Interpretation of Tongues (our own or others)

We can receive a message from the voice of God through interpretation of tongues, privately in our prayer closet or publicly in a local church service.

This is another gift of the Spirit (1Corinthians 12:10) and works in conjunction with the gift of speaking in tongues. (If you would like to know more about tongues and interpretation of tongues I recommend my book, "On the Subject of Tongues," available in paperback or Kindle on www.Amazon.com). Tongues with interpretation is equal to the gift of prophecy in that they both edify and build up the body of Christ. Paul said, "I wish you all spoke with tongues, but even more that you prophesied; for he who prophesies is greater than he who speaks with tongues, unless indeed he interprets, that the church may receive edification" (1Corinthians 14:5, NKJV). Tongues with interpretation will not only build up your faith but it will build up the faith of the congregation too! Faith comes by hearing God speak.

21. The Audible Voice of God

God spoke to Moses audibly, or face-to-face (Numbers 12:8). Isaiah records these words of promise to Believers, "Your ears shall hear a word behind you, saying, 'This is the way, walk in it,' whenever you turn to the right hand or whenever you turn to the left" (Isaiah 30:21, NKJV). God guides us in many ways; including the audible voice of the Holy Spirit. God's audible voice, however, is usually reserved for situations involving dangers that need immediate attention to preserve life, or to prepare us for something that we wouldn't have the faith to stand against unless we heard him speak to us audibly. When He

speaks in this manner, it is startling to say the least and can, at times, even be terrifying. God doesn't often speak in this manner, but if He speaks to you this way, instant obedience is the best response and might be required.

22. Through Animals

Can God speak through an animal? He is God of all creation and if we don't praise Him, He will strike the rocks and they will cry out. If a rock can cry out why can't an animal speak in a man's voice? This is exactly what happened to the rebellious prophet Balaam. "Then the Lord opened the mouth of the donkey, and she said to Balaam, 'What have I done to you, that you have struck me these three times?'" (Numbers 22:28, NKJV). We can't limit God.

If it's recorded in the Bible, it's recorded for our learning. "For whatever things were written before were written for our learning, that we through the patience and comfort of the Scriptures might have hope" (Romans 15:4, NKJV).

I'm not saying we should try to become like the fictional storybook character Doctor Doolittle and begin speaking to animals, but at the same time, if God chooses to speak through a donkey, or a human being we consider to be a type of donkey, we should take heed to the voice within the voice of the one speaking. At the same time, it's wise to remember, the devil spoke through a serpent in the Garden of Eden and deceived God's children. Therefore, it's always wise to test the spirits on every voice before obeying any instructions (see also 1John 4:4-6).

23. Through Other People

God often uses other people to speak to us. Pastors, parents, teachers, wives, husbands, etc. God even speaks to us out of the mouths of babes.

Age is not a prerequisite for God to speak through an individual. In fact, the only one of Job's friends that spoke God's truth was Elihu, the youngest of the group. He said, "I am young in years, and you are very old; therefore, I was afraid and dared not declare my opinion to you. I said, 'Age should speak, and multitude of years should teach wisdom.'

But there is a spirit in man, and the breath of the Almighty gives him understanding (Job 32:6-8, NKJV). I encourage you to claim the promise from Isaiah, "The Lord God has given Me the tongue of the learned, that I should know how to speak a word in season to him who is weary" (Isaiah 50:4, NKJV). God wants to speak to others through you. "If anyone speaks, let him speak as the oracles of God.

If anyone ministers, let him do it as with the ability which God supplies, that in all things God may be glorified through Jesus Christ" (1Peter 4:11, NKJV). The key is taking time to sit at His feet and listen. Be prepared to hear God through the words of other people, bringing refreshment from the Holy Spirit and the Father's heart. "Everyone enjoys giving good advice, and how wonderful it is

to be able to say the right thing at the right time!" (Proverbs 15:23, LVB). Let's not forget that the devil speaks through people also, false prophets, false teachers, and even friends and family members. Job's wife spoke the very words of Satan during their time of trouble, "Then his wife said to him, 'Do you still hold to your integrity? Curse God and die!'" (Job 2:9, NKJV). Test the spirits on everything you hear. You have the Holy Spirit of truth. Rely upon Him to confirm or refute whatever is spoken to you through others as you continue to grow in Christ.

24. In Response to Our Own Idols

This one startles me. God will allow us to be deceived if we come to a prophet of the Lord with idols in our heart.

And the word of the Lord came to me, saying, "'Son of man, these men have set up their idols in their hearts, and put before them that which causes them to stumble into iniquity. Should I let Myself be inquired of at all by them? Therefore speak to them, and say to them, 'Thus says the Lord God: Everyone of the house of Israel who sets up his idols in his heart, and puts before him what causes him to stumble into iniquity, and then comes to the prophet, I the Lord will answer him who comes, according to the multitude of his idols.'" (Ezekiel 14:2-4, NKJV)

Said another way, God will give us the answer our own idolatrous desires are crying out for, leading us into a bad relationship, business deal, or other decision to teach us a lesson. Because of this we should ask God to reveal any hidden sin in our lives first, and then, seek Him for revelation. He will then cleanse us from any idols, things we desire above the Lord's desires.

King David prayed, "Who can understand his errors? **Cleanse me from secret faults**. Keep back Your servant also from presumptuous sins; Let them not have dominion over me. Then I shall be blameless, And I shall be innocent of great transgression" (Psalms 19:12-13, NKJV). King David made some mistakes, but because he continued to go before the Lord for cleansing the Bible records, he was "a man after God's own heart" (Acts 13:22). I want to be recorded the same way. This can only come through seeking God in the same manner as King David did. Otherwise, we will be full of idols and God will send us "strong delusion that we might believe a lie" (2Thessalonians 2:10-11). Scripture says the only reason God does this is "because we received not the love of the truth" (v. 12) in the first place. As you move forward in your desire to hear from God first begin by repenting from any unconfessed sin. Ask the Holy Spirit to remove from you any secret faults and presumptuous sins. Then move forward in faith. "God opposes the proud but gives grace to the humble" (1Peter 5:5, RSV).

25. Through False Prophets to "Test Us"

Again, God will test us in our commitment to Him by allowing false prophets to prophesy an accurate sign or wonder that actually comes to pass. Then the false prophet will tell us to follow after **other gods**, false gods, to lead us away from Jesus." "If there arises among you a prophet or a dreamer of dreams, and he gives you a sign or a wonder, and the sign or the wonder of which he spoke to you comes to pass, saying, 'Let us go after other gods which you have not known, and let us serve them,' you shall not listen to the words of that prophet or that dreamer of dreams, for the Lord your God is testing you to know whether you love the Lord your God with all your heart and with all your soul. You shall walk after the Lord your God and fear Him, and keep His commandments and obey His voice, and you shall serve Him and hold fast to Him" (Deuteronomy 13:1-4, NKJV). (See also 2Chronicles 18:1-25, where God sends a deceiving spirit to become "a lying spirit in the mouths of all Ahab's prophets," to lead him to his own destruction in battle.)

Staying focused on Jesus and His Word will enable us to pass the false prophet test every time and empower us to deliver others from following false gods that cannot save. Jesus says, "My sheep hear (obey) my voice and they follow me" (John 10:27).

CONCLUSION

God speaks in **many ways**. In fact, Scripture also records God speaking through parables (Matthew 13:1-52), riddles (Ezekiel 17:2), music (Psalms 49:4), puns (Matthew 23:24), supernatural handwriting on the wall (Dan. 5:5), showing of hard sentences (Daniel 5:12), dissolving of doubts (Daniel 5:12), conundrums (Psalms 49:4), and signs in the sky (Acts 2:19). When testing the spirits with all revelation we receive, it is imperative that we remember that God's spoken voice will always line up with His Written Voice in Scripture. God never speaks anything that doesn't line up with the 66 books of the Bible.

However, God has no problem speaking something that is contrary to our own **interpretation** of Scripture. Remember the Pharisees? They studied the Scriptures daily and then rejected Jesus, the Word made Flesh, when He arrived on the scene even though He clearly fulfilled the very Scriptures they had studied about His coming. Since we have their lives as a warning example, let's not make a similar mistake. Instead, let's always remain open to receive the voice of God speaking through the agent of the Holy Spirit, the Spirit of Truth that Jesus said He would be sending to us for this very purpose. "However, when He, the Spirit of truth, has come, He will guide you into all truth; for He will not speak on His own authority, but whatever He hears He will speak; **and He will tell you things to come**" (John 16:13, NKJV). The Holy Spirit is communicating the very words of Jesus to us in various ways every day. Let us continue to seek God that we might more accurately and effectively hear His voice amidst all the other voices of the world that are constantly vying for our attention. Once we know it is God speaking to us, may He enable us to obey what He tells us to do. Remember the key to unleashing the miraculous? **"Whatever He says to you, do it"** (John 2:5, NKJV)!

7 KEYS TO PROPERLY HEARING GOD

The following is a brief listing of 7 Keys to Properly Hearing God. Utilizing these keys will help place us in a proper position to hear from Heaven.

Key # 1 – Stay in His Presence

By cultivating the presence of the Lord in our lives, we become more acutely aware of God speaking to us. Our ability to distinguish his voice from all the other voices of the world increases. This occurs organically as we spend consistent time with Him in devotions. Genuine prayer is a dialogue (two-way communication, us speaking to God and God speaking back to us. He releases and imparts His love, truth, knowledge, wisdom, understanding, plans, wisdom, and timing, as well as instruction, directives and when necessary, correction (see Psalm 91).

Key # 2 – Focus on God's Purposes

By cultivating an ever-increasing commitment to the purposes of God, we effectively position ourselves to hear and receive prophetic insight and revelation from Him. Amos 3:7 says that God will "do nothing except He first reveal it to His servants, the prophets." When we grow in the prophetic gifts God will speak to us, at times, as a man speaks to his friend. God will share things with us for people's highest good. In prayer each do we should inquire of Him to reveal His plan and our part or partnership is releasing His will into the situation. Then we too can say as spiritual sons of God, "Most assuredly, I say to you, the

Son can do nothing of Himself, but what He sees the Father do; for whatever He does, the Son also does in like manner" (John 5:19, NKJV).

Key # 3 – Persistent Asking, Seeking and Knocking

God loves when we are eager and hungry for more of Him and to have our hearts filled with his love to help others. God says he desires to give us the Kingdom (Luke 12:32). If we ask the Lord for prophetic insight or revelation in order to minister to others, He will often speak to us (see Jeremiah 33:3; Colossians 1:9-13; Ephesians 3:13-20). Jesus himself directed us to "ask, seek, and knock" (Matthew 7:7). The New Testament was written in the Greek language; these three words are in what is referred to as the **present imperative tense**. The *present imperative* tense denotes "a command to do something now, with a **constant repeated action** in the future." This means that Jesus is not only directing us to ask, seek, and knock, but to do so continually. This passage could be better translated, "ASK (and keep on asking) and it will be given to you, SEEK (and keep on seeking), and you will find, KNOCK (and keep on knocking) and the door will be opened unto you" (Matthew 7:7). Asking God continually is a powerful key to receiving from the Lord. (See also Jesus' example of the persistent widow, who with her persistent asking received her request from the King (Luke 18:1-10).

Key # 4 – Growing in Love Towards God and Others

The Spiritual Gifts are given so that we can effectively minister God's grace to others (1Corinthians 12:7-8). True discernment is generated from a place of Godly love (Philippians 1:9). As a greater measure of God's love develops and grows in us for others, he will release greater and more accurate prophetic revelation. By simply asking God to fill us with a deeper measure of His love for people can help accelerate this process. *"Faith works by love"* (Galatians 5:6).

Key # 5 – Perform a Spiritual Body Check

It's important to remember that God speaks through all five spiritual senses (spiritual smell, touch, taste, as well as sight and hearing). Because of this, it is wise to do what is referred to by many prophetic people as a spiritual "body check." When you do you might discover that God is giving you an impression in your spirit, soul, or body. If this occurs, and it often will if you are paying attention, you are best positioned to hear God speak through this avenue of communication.

Key # 6 – The Power of Prayer and Fasting

Isaiah chapter 58 promises us that prayer and fasting will release God's answer to our cry (v. 8), and that the Lord will guide us continually (v. 11). Fasting is not required for your salvation, you are saved by grace through faith alone, not of works lest any man should boast (Ephesians 2:8-9). But if you want to see the highest will of God released from heaven in and through your life and the lives of those around you, fasting is the key. Certain breakthroughs only occur through prayer and fasting combined (see Mark 9:29 KJV).

Jesus told his disciples that certain things can only be accomplished through the combination of prayer and fasting (see Mark 9:29, Matthew 17:21 KJV). Fasting not only strengthens our spirit to hear from God, but it also weakens the voice of our flesh and every other voice that vies for our attention in this life. Through fasting and prayer, you'll tune into God's voice as King amidst the Seven voices in this world.

Key # 7 – The Power of God's Written Word

The Bible is our "more sure word of prophecy" (2Peter 1:19-21). If we love God's written word and feed our soul on it, we will begin to **grow in our sensitivity** to His spoken word as well. This will also enable us to hear Him more clearly when He communicates through "dark sayings" or "in riddles" that need interpretation (Number 12:8, KJV). When we are faithful with God's written Word the Holy Spirit will illuminate our understanding and bring into remembrance all things that God has spoken to us (John 14:26). I encourage you to seek God daily through His written Word and trust Him to add all these other things unto you over time. "He who is faithful with little, will be given authority over much" (see Matthew 25:21).

By making these 7 Disciplines a part of our lives, we will begin to grow in our sensitivity to the various ways God speaks. As we grow, we will be amazed at how clearly, we can receive revelation we previously did not notice. When we begin more consistently recognize His voice, we can then begin developing our ability to interpret the prophetic revelation (information) we receive. Then we can begin asking God for wisdom for proper application and benefit for those whom He has given us revelation and interpretation.

FINAL PRAYER

Heavenly Father, thank you for sending Jesus to speak to us 2,000 years ago. Jesus, thank you for sending the Holy Spirit to guide us personally, into all truth so that we might be changed into the image and likeness of the Son of God. Holy Spirit, I ask you to tune the ears of my spirit to hear You when You speak whatever you hear from Jesus. I ask You to make it so clear that not even a fool can misunderstand. I thank You for telling and showing me the things to come, as Jesus promises You will. Today, I ask You to enroll me in the School of the Holy Spirit that I may learn to hear and obey the voice of God. I ask this in Jesus' Mighty Name. Amen.

May you become one who hears His voice and releases His kingdom wherever He sends you! Your future is bright!

Shalom, Shalom,

David C. Hairabedian

David and Joanna Hairabedian are co-founders of VirtualChurchMedia.com. They live in Southern, California. David is an author, teacher and conference speaker.

Joanna is a writer, singer, and Prophetic Psalmist. Together, they host a weekly TV Broadcast called, In His Presence, Where ALL Things are Possible. David teaches and Joanna plays piano and sings. People report receiving encouragement, deliverance, healing and a tangible Presence of the Lord while watching these programs.

To download our free ministry mobile app and access Quantum

Christianity, ministry on demand, from the palm of your hand, visit www.VirtualChurchMedia.com.

Contact Information or

To make a donation or to partner:

Virtual Church Media Inc

1835 Newport Blvd

Building A-109, #333

Costa Mesa, CA 92627

(949) 648-1699

Info@VirtualChurchMedia.com

Prayer@VirtualChurchMedia.com

www.VirtualChurchMedia.com

To purchase a copy of David's critically acclaimed autobiography, ***Jet Ride to Hell, Journey to Freedom***, visit VirtualChurchMedia.com or go to Amazon.com

"Arrested with a Stolen Jet - David is a critically acclaimed author, speaker, and lead pastor. His autobiography "Jet Ride to Hell, Journey to Freedom" tells of his incredible transformation story – one that exemplifies God's beautiful plan of redemption and grace. David was a convicted felon, where he spent 20 years in federal prison for stealing multi-million-dollar jet aircraft for the Colombian drug cartel. However, a life's path that seemed to have stamped a one-way ticket to hell was dramatically changed by a mother's prayer and a faithful God. A riveting storyline that includes a sting operation carried out by 20-armed federal agents on the tarmac of a South Florida runway, and the tales of a prisoner living inside America's maximum-security prison, Leavenworth Penitentiary – this autobiography will captivate you from start to finish!"

To learn more about how you can *Help change lives, one Bible at a Time*, or making a difference by supporting Bibles for prisoners visit www.HeartPrisonMinistries.org. Partnering with Jesus to Help Raise up 12 Disciples a Year through our Bible a month program can be life-changing for the prisoner as well as the one who gives to make it possible.

Visit to learn more how you can be the answer to someone's prayers.

For additional teachings, video sermonettes, Christian resource materials, ministry updates, visit these sites:

- ✓ www.VirtualChurchTV.com
- ✓ www.HeartPrisonMinistries.org
- ✓ www.DavidHairabedian.com

You are Fools for Christ by David C. Hairabedian

The Apostle Paul said he and the other apostles were fools for Christ. In this thought-provoking book, you'll discover you are either a fool for Christ or a fool for someone or something else. The good news is You get to choose. Question? Whose fool are you? Daring to be a fool for Christ will result in a life well lived; one that brings miracles from Heaven through your daring obedience into the earth. This book will take you to the next level!

What the Bible REALLY says about Speaking in Tongues, by David C. Hairabedian.

Discover what the Word of God has to say about the gift of tongues. Pastor David Hairabedian guides you through this subject sharing from his own personal experience and through a topical study based on the Word of God.

Permitting and Prohibiting: You get to choose!

By David C. Hairabedian

Discover your authority to open the doors to heaven and close the gates of hell.

"There is a Spiritual Key for Every Healing," was the words I heard as the vision opened before my eyes. Then I was shown the "spiritual keys" that unlocked the doors for healing and miracles of almost every kind for man, woman, and child. In this book, you will receive the "key" or "keys" you've been looking for that will open the door to your breakthrough, healing, miracle, relationship restoration, and even your destiny. Discover how God has already been speaking to you and simultaneously receive the faith to step out to accomplish your purposes in the earth. This book is a must read!

Hope Deferred Makes the Heart Sick, Proverbs 13:12

Overcoming Disappointment and achieving Victory by David C. Hairabedian. (Book 2 in the Freedom from Bondage Series) This poignant book reveals the three-phase strategy of Hope Deferred:

1). Life's very real circumstances that contradict the promises of God

2) Negative mindset that develops that is contrary to the Word of God.

3) A Demon spirit that comes to oppress our minds and sicken our hearts against God.

(Proverbs 13:12): "Hope deferred makes the heart sick, but a longing fulfilled is a tree of life.

The Six Stages of Hope Deferred 1) Disillusioned, 2) Confusion, 3) Unbelief, 4) Disillusionment 5) Bitterness, and 6) Cynicism.

Inside this book, you will find HOPE and experience breakthrough. Many experience deliverance and breakthrough while reading this book and praying the prayer in the final chapter. Also, a great gift for a friend in need of this message.

Twelve Supernatural Healing Vehicles from God's Word: Different Ways God Heals Today! (Freedom From Bondage Series, Book 12)

Seven Deadly Diseases of the Tongue. Learn about the seven deadly diseases of the tongue. Each one can greatly affect your life, relationships, and destiny. All can lead to "foot in mouth disease." Discover the strategic way the Bible teaches to protect yourself from yourself, and simultaneously purge your mouth from any remaining viper venom.

The wisest Old Testament king penned these words, "Death and life are in the power of the tongue" (Proverbs 18:21). The New Testament author declared, "No man can tame the tongue, it is a restless evil and full of deadly poison" (James 3:7). But there is supernatural hope for you. Inside this book, you will receive the spiritual keys to control your tongue and the roadmap to receiving heaven's empowerment for a new tongue that will enable you to overcome every obstacle in your path. A must read for those who really want victory.

"No one goes to hell by accident!" were the words I heard as the vision opened before me. The scenes that followed forever changed the way I saw the often-controversial subject of Hell. This experience confirmed that hell is a real place. It also served to confirm it is very difficult to go to hell, although many will end up there. You have to work at it. Jesus is constantly getting in your path to redirect you to Heaven. The Bible records hundreds of Scriptures about hell. Jesus spoke more about hell than Heaven. This book is a quick ready and will empower you to know the truth that will ensure your ticket to heaven. A must read for every man, woman, and child. No one goes to hell by accident! By David C. Hairabedian

Jet Ride to Hell, Journey to Freedom, by David Hairabedian, 372 pages.

The true, riveting story that includes a sting operation carried out by 20-armed federal agents on the tarmac of a South Florida runway, and the tales of a prisoner serving a 20 year sentence and living inside America's maximum security prison, Leavenworth Penitentiary – this autobiography will captivate you from start to finish. A redemption story filled with miracles, signs and heavenly encounters that inspire and spark faith in the reader to experience the same things from God. Five stars!

Dealing with Demons by David Hairabedian, 56 Pages.

This book helps identify the cause of many of our problems in life, from work to personal, addictions, relational and tormenting dreams and thoughts. Between the covers of this powerful book you will find information and revelation that leads to freedom, power packed with Scripture to support every page.

Hearing God 25 Different Biblical Ways by David Hairabedian, 53 pages.

Do you ever wonder why your relationship with God feels stale? Have you ever wished you could just hear if God was saying something -- anything -- to you? Grow in your relationship with God as you learn about the many ways God uses to communicate with you! Inside this book you'll discover God has already been speaking to you. Now you are listening and can obey what He says. This book is life-changing for the reader and helps launch them into a life of "hearing and obeying" the voice of the Holy Spirit. A must read for every hungry seeker after God.

Points to Ponder: (Questions about Healing the Sick and Miracles today) by David Hairabedian, 30 pages.

This poignant and thought-provoking book will answer the numerous questions that many have asked. "Does God heal and do miracles today? If so, why aren't we seeing these in and through our lives and ministries? Why aren't our prayers being answered in the same ways?" This book will distinguish between "Modern Churchianity" and "Biblicial Christianity." By the time you are done reading this book you'll begin praying biblically and seeing Biblical manifestations and answers to prayer. Praying "thy kingdom come, thy will be done, in earth as it is in heaven" will bring on whole new meaning and results in an encounter with God. We dare you to read this book! Your life will never be the same!

FOCUS AND GOALS
"Where Your Success Journey Begins"
5/25 Rule

The 5/25 Rule is a valuable exercise to help map. out your goals. This process will enable you to identify your priorities and eliminate distractions. Clearly identifying the top priorities will help you achieve your goals and be focused.

STEP 1

List twenty-five things you want to accomplish in life. Nothing is too big or small.

Rank order	List Top 25 Goals	Rank Order	List Top 25 Goals

FOCUS AND GOALS
"Where Your Success Journey Begins"
5/25 Rule

STEP 2
Rank the top five goals in the order of importance. (1 is the most important) Fill in the "rank order" box column. Then circle the top five.

STEP 3
Draw a line through the rest of the 20 priorities. These are distractions until you have completed and succeeded with your top 5 priorities.

STEP 4
Once the five priorities are successfully completed, re-assess and then repeat the process.

STEP 5
Every time you accomplish a goal, pick something to reward yourself. For example, buy yourself something that you've been wanting, spa treatment, clothing item, etc.

A ship with a compass and map sets the course to achieve its destination. Setting your goals and priorities with the 5/25 Rule is your path that will lead to a fulfilled life of achieving your dreams and destiny.

CONGRATULATIONS on making the decision to set your course for great things!

FOCUS AND GOALS
"Where Your Success Journey Begins"
5/25 Rule

Copyright © 2019 VirtualChurchMedia.com
All Rights Reserved | David and Joanna Hairabedian

FOCUS AND GOALS
"Where Your Success Journey Begins"
5/25 Rule

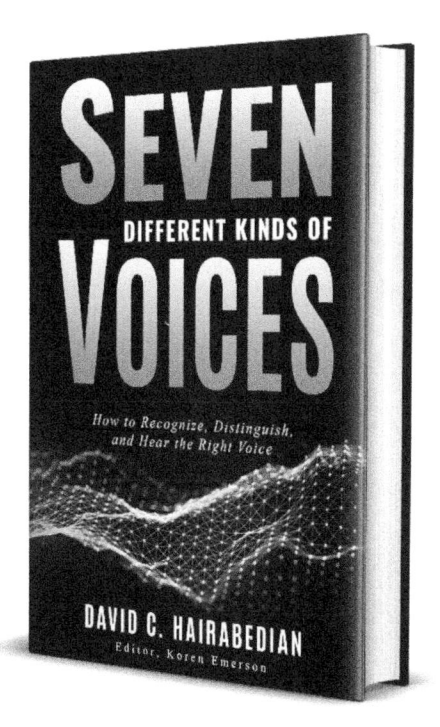

Copyright © 2019 VirtualChurchMedia.com
All Rights Reserved | David and Joanna Hairabedian

Made in the USA
Monee, IL
08 July 2021